Difficult Normativity

Jan-Olav Henriksen (ed.)

Difficult Normativity

Normative Dimensions in Research on Religion and Theology

PETER LANG
Frankfurt am Main · Berlin · Bern · Bruxelles · New York · Oxford · Wien

Bibliographic Information published by the Deutsche Nationalbibliothek
The Deutsche Nationalbibliothek lists this publication in the Deutsche Nationalbibliografie; detailed bibliographic data is available in the internet at http://dnb.d-nb.de.

Cover Design:
© Olaf Glöckler, Atelier Platen, Friedberg

ISBN 978-3-631-61993-3
© Peter Lang GmbH
Internationaler Verlag der Wissenschaften
Frankfurt am Main 2011
All rights reserved.

All parts of this publication are protected by copyright. Any utilisation outside the strict limits of the copyright law, without the permission of the publisher, is forbidden and liable to prosecution. This applies in particular to reproductions, translations, microfilming, and storage and processing in electronic retrieval systems.

www.peterlang.de

Table of Contents

Contributors 7

Acknowledgements 9

Introduction
Jan-Olav Henriksen 11

Normative dimensions in empirical research on religion, values and society
Jan-Olav Henriksen 17

Empirical research and theological normativity
Ulla Schmidt 37

Normative evaluations in theological ethics
Paul Leer-Salvesen 65

Normativity and empirical data in practical theology
Harald Hegstad 77

The non-confessional study of religion and its normative dimensions
Ingvild Sælid Gilhus 95

Normativity in empirical social studies
Ole Riis 109

Cultural empirical studies and normativity: A case from missiology
Kari Storstein Haug 131

Contributors

Ingvild Sælid Gilhus is professor of religious studies at the University of Bergen, Norway.

Harald Hegstad is professor of systematic theology at (MF) Norwegian School of Theology, Oslo.

Jan-Olav Henriksen is professor of philosophy of religion at (MF) Norwegian School of Theology, Oslo; professor of religious studies at the University of Agder, Norway, and director of the Norwegian Research School *Religion Values Society.*

Paul Leer-Salvesen is professor of theology and ethics at the University of Agder, Kristiansand, Norway.

Ole Riis is professor of sociology of religion at the University of Agder, Kristiansand, Norway.

Ulla Schmidt is acting Director of Research at the Centre for Church research in Oslo, and professor of ethics at the Faculty of Theology, University of Oslo.

Kari Storstein Haug is associate professor of Missiology at the School of Mission and Theology, Stavanger, Norway.

Acknowledgements

I would like to extend my expression of gratitude to the following persons who have contributed in different ways to this volume. First of all, the PhD-students of the Norwegian Research School Religion Values Society (RS RVS) who participated in the course we had on normativity and empirical research in Metochi, Lesvos in the summer of 2010. Their responses to the lecturers' contributions were of great importance to what would later be made into articles dealing with the different and difficult dimensions of normativity.

Second, I would like to thank all those who have contributed to this volume, first by participating in the course and giving lectures, and then by turning the lectures into articles. In addition, I extend a thank you to professors Ingvild Sælid Gilhus and Ulla Schmidt, who supplemented the participating lecturers' work with contributions from their point of view – and based on their experience with some of the topics. This added to the common effort of scholars from many different institutions in Norway that made the book possible.

Finally, a thank you to Irene Tvedt Wangen, PhD, who at the time of the course was the secretary of the RS RVS, and who took care of all practical matters involved in making it a successful and pleasant event. Together with the wonderful staff at Metochi, she made us realize that it is indeed possible to combine hard work, pleasant circumstances, and good fellowship during the days we spent there.

Oslo, June, 2011

Jan-Olav Henriksen

Director, RS RVS

Introduction

Jan-Olav Henriksen

Over the last 20-30 years there has been a considerable shift in the ways many PhD-studies in theology and religious studies have been designed. Moving from projects mainly based on texts, or the study of different ritual practices, we have observed an increasing number of projects dealing with empirical material, be it observations based upon field work, or interviews, or analysis of different expressions not necessarily related to what has traditionally been considered religious (like what one can find in popular culture). This change makes it possible to claim that the shift towards a methodology rooted in the social sciences that took place in many other disciplines in the 1970s and 1980, is now also taking place in the field of religious studies and theology.

The following example illustrates this new situation: when establishing a new doctoral program in 1991, none of the projects admitted by the Norwegian School of Theology were empirically based. 30 years later, approximately half of them are empirical. The same is probably the case in many other similar institutions, not only in Norway, but around the world. In the long run this will probably have some impact on how theology and religious studies are shaped as scholarly disciplines.

However, reflections are still somewhat lacking when it comes to what this strong empirical turn means for considering some of the basic theoretical features in the design of research projects in theology and religious studies. The present book is a result of experiences we had when the Norwegian Research School *Religion Values Society* offered a course for PhD-students at Metochi Study Center in Greece in August 2010: We realized that very little had been written that dealt comprehensively with the normative dimensions of doing research on topics related to the field of this research school.[1] This may be surprising at first glance, but taking the

---

1 There are some exceptions, though, in this volume mainly present in references made in the article by Kari Storstein Haug. There have also been some reflections about the value dimensions in such research, e.g., in a conference in Denmark in 1998, documented in Lars Albinus, Armin W. Geertz, and Peter Widmann: (Eds.): *Værdier i religionsforskning og religionsundervisning i Danmark.* Århus: Det Teologiske fakultet, Århus universitet, 2001. However, as I suggest below, one should not immediately identify the value dimension with the normative dimension in the types of research we are addressing in the present volume.

following into consideration, it might not be: In theology, the assumption that theology is an – at least partly normative – discipline has been a taken for granted. Thus, one has not seen the need for developing this assumption further. On the other hand, the situation in religious studies has been the opposite, but taken for granted in the same way: religious studies have been considered a discipline without any traits of normative grounding (much opposed to what is the case in theology, as one can see from Ingvild Gilhus' article below). It does not require much reflection, however, in order to realize that there are a lot of different dimensions of normativity hidden within both disciplines; dimensions that make it important to consider more in detail how and why we may talk about and understand the normative dimensions of theology and religious studies.

As the present book documents, there is a cluster of different dimensions of normativity related to studying religion from an empirical point of view. For analytical purposes, we may list them in the following manner (there may be different combinations of the following features, as well as overlaps):

- The normativity of research design: This includes both the choices of what to investigate, by which conceptual and theoretical means, and for what purpose,
- The normativity of research ethics: This includes both Merton's identification of basic scholarly or scientific norms (cf. below 112f.), but also norms related to how to deal with the concerns of informants or delicate material,
- The normativity that has to do with the impact of the study done in a wider social context,
- The theological normativities – where empirical studies are also taken to have some relevance for what is considered a theologically valid (normatively accepted / acceptable) position,
- The normativity behind a position that assumes that it is possible to have a neutral or inter-subjective stand over against questions dealt with within the field of religion and society,
- The institutional and political normativities: These may be partly related to research ethics, partly to theological convictions, and partly to what counts as good research within a university. Included here may also be the potential allegiances the researcher has toward a religious, political or other institution.

The above list is not exhaustive. The reader of this book may realize that many of the authors address more than one of these dimensions in the following. He or she may also observe that a list like the above contains more than an identification of potential *values* that may be implied in empirical research on religion / theology. This is testimony to the fact that a lot of the difficult normativities that are inherent in this field of research cannot be easily defined as values. Instead, they are also linked to guiding principles of conduct, to normative rules, or doctrinal decisions which there may be more to than what we normally speak of as values. While values are always contextual and related to specific cultural conditions, the normativity that may be inherent in scholarly work *per definition* implies a claim for their potential validity even outside of such contexts and conditions. This is then related to the claims for universality and "communism" (Merton) or inter-subjectivity that constitutes all scholarly work.

What all the contributions to this volume have in common, though, is the conviction that it is impossible to do studies in religion and society without engaging with some– or all of – these normative dimensions. Hence, the following can be read as an argument for the position that there is a normative dimension is all studies that investigate empirical dimensions of religion, values, and society. As scholars, we are part of that which we study, and a neutral and positivistic stance that does not reflect any kind of normative convictions is not possible.

The insistence on a necessary normative dimension is only one side of the coin, however: the other side is the claim that without being aware of these necessary normative dimensions, they may tend to determine the field of studies in ways that are not desirable. It is only by being aware of the different dimensions of normativity in empirical studies that students of theology and religion will be able to handle the impact of these normative dimensions in a transparent – and accordingly – scholarly way. Because the normative dimensions make the study difficult when it comes to how to assess them, the primary goal when dealing with the difficult normativities is to articulate them and explicate them in a transparent way in order to make them discussable. That is a basic requirement for scholarly work, and for understanding how the empirical dimension that is investigated relates to, and is shaped by, implicit or explicit normative elements that guide the empirical material studied.

A way to enter the question about the relation between normativity and empirical description which is not explicitly addressed in this volume, but which may be worth considering, is related to looking at normativity vs. empirical by distinguishing between explanation and understanding /

interpretation when analyzing a given material. This approach may shed additional light on the topic. Given that empirical material can also be *explained* by causes that do not necessarily involve any direct normative stance, one may ask if such material is not reduced more than what is appropriate if we do not also engage it within a horizon that has to do with its impact for understanding human behavior and agency. A horizon like the latter, though, implies interpretation and decisions as to what matters more, and to whom. Although the contributions here, as previously indicated, do not explicitly reflect on this distinction and its impact on the theme, one may nevertheless say that many of the following contributions try to reconcile this dichotomy by engaging in a specific type of hermeneutics that deliberately opens up for considering the pragmatic context and dimensions of this kind of research. Such hermeneutics, in turn, tries to bridge the divide between explanation and understanding.

Furthermore, as normativity is not a mere "out there", but always indicates a relation between researcher and the object of her research, any consideration about normativity and empirical research also implies some kind of self-reflection on the part of the researcher. Hence, we should not only ask in what way normativity is part of how the unit of analysis is constituted – we also need to ask how and in what ways normativities constitute the *subject* of research and the community in which she participates. Without knowledge of such elements, we have a far less transparent understanding of normativity in play.

The following contributions address the hermeneutical and theoretical implications given with the discourses about the relation between empirical material and normativity, more than they discuss theories that emerge out of specific theoretical positions with inherent normativites as such. The reason is simply that the latter are part of the theoretical repertoire of religious studies, while *we here focus more on normativity given in or related to the design of research projects*. Some hints toward what is here described as missing may nevertheless be found in Ole Riis' discussion of critical theory. Accordingly, the focus in this volume implies that none of the following contributions go thoroughly into theoretical approaches like the one offered by e.g., Michel Foucault, in order to find out what such an approach would mean to the topics discussed here. Also, there is no explicit discussion about what other types of critique of religion and religious studies may offer when it comes to assessing religion (and values) critically from a given and normative point of view. To go into such dimensions of normativity would expand the scope of the present book beyond its limits. Our aim is more modest: to present students who work with empirical material within the disciplines of theology and religious studies with material for reflection about what I, in the following article below, call constitutive normativity.

In conclusion, then, this book should be read as offering resources for making students in the different scholarly fields of theology and religion more aware of *what* normativity is at work, and *how* it is at work, when they develop their research. As one will see, the following chapters combine examples from recent research practice (often by the authors themselves, and not only success stories) with more theoretical considerations. This exemplifies the combination that every scholar needs to handle in order to make transparent how she deals with the difficulties of normativity.

Normative dimensions in empirical research on religion, values and society

Jan-Olav Henriksen

Introduction

The argument in the following rests on a basic conviction: an understanding of the relation between the empirical or descriptive and the normative elements in research cannot be neatly divided in a manner that implies the following model:

a) Description of empirical data that is considered to be objective and neutral, +
b) Normative elements, which are more or less arbitrary, subjective, and *added on to* the already and independently established descriptive level of research =
c) The totality of research, which allows us to both have an objective and a more normative or value-based assessment of what is the case.

I will argue that to apply a model like this one to human and social sciences is wrong from the very outset, and will exemplify the basic philosophical points for this argument by substantiating it with further references to some points from theology and religious studies. The argument will have some relevance for what other contributors to this book present when they deal with the position of David Hume.

This presentation will have two main parts. In the first part, I will deal with some basic elements from philosophy and hermeneutics, which aim to make problematic a clear-cut and easy-made distinction between normativity and empirical description. The aim of this first part is not to blur any such distinctions or say that they are not relevant; they are. The aim is to point to the fact that there is more implied in, and hidden behind, this distinction than what may be discerned initially. Hopefully, this will then serve as a means for a better analytical grip on the topic and serve as a backdrop for some of what may be said in later lectures.

The second section of this presentation will then, as suggested, go more detailed into implicit and explicit normative elements in research that may be relevant to consider for ethics, theology and religious studies. Although the examples will be taken from these disciplines, I will suggest that what is said may also be of importance to discussion in other disciplines, such as pedagogy and psychology – probably also to sociology. How well and how far I will be able to develop such relevance remains to be seen.

Basic philosophical considerations

Let us start in a simple way: The first thing you have to do in research is to constitute your object of analysis. This means that what you are going to do research on is never merely given. It has to be identified, delineated and established by means of theory. All these elements demand decisions. Sometimes, such decisions are made beforehand by the research community that has already established a specific way of analyzing and understanding certain phenomena and / or problems (cf. Thomas Kuhn's notion of the paradigms that make regular or ordinary science work), but sometimes you will also have to make some decisions yourself, as to how you find it most appropriate to establish your object of analysis.

My point at this stage is not simply to say that by making such decisions, you are also making a normative claim (although this is also an important point). The normative claim this point implies, can be formulated as follows:

N^1: When doing research on topic X with regard to Y, *we are best served* by understanding it from the (theoretical) perspective of Z.

This is a claim that, as stated here, appears to be evaluative ("best served"), and contains a kind of implicit recommendation as to how to proceed. We will return to that in a moment, but let us also note that this is not first and foremost (or at all) an evaluative component that you add to the material that you have described or aim to analyze, rather, this is a way of constituting (normatively) the object that you are aiming to analyze. Hence, there is, already at this stage, a type of *constitutive* normativity implied here.

This type of *constitutive normativity* is implied in all research. The very concepts we use, and the obligation we take on when we are to use them in a precise manner, is in itself also normative in character. We take on the responsibility to be coherent, precise, consistent and verifiable / repeatable (depending on topic). There are basic elements in research ethics – and I will not deal with them here, just make the point that without such an ethic, research is probably not possible to engage in, in a meaningful way: This is what makes research possible to discuss and possible to see as presenting claims for validity. Unless these basic normative elements are present, we are not dealing with research, but with the art of writing fiction. Hence, we may say that these are normative conditions for making scholarly descriptions.

Let us – after this small interlude – have another look at N^1: As stated above, it is clear that there is a normative element in N^1 that implies some recommendations with regard to theory and procedure / perspective. But this does not mean that N^1 is only a normative claim. How normativity and description is linked we can see clearly if we re-formulate N^1 into version N^2:

N^2: *It is the case that* research on topic X with regard to Y is best served by understanding it from the (theoretical) perspective of Z.

This reformulation helps us to focus our attention on two more points: First, there is a claim here as to what is the case in the research undertaken. Such claims about what is the case are usually considered major components of the descriptive component of research – but here we should remember that we are talking about the *constitution* of the research object – and not a statement about what is the case with regards to this object as such (when understanding X with regard to Y from the perspective of Z). In other words: this is a claim about what is the case with regard to how to constitute the object – not a claim about an object already constituted (which in turn is then of course the object of analysis).

Furthermore, the formulation of N^2 helps us see that in evaluation, a *comparative* element is involved. When stating that it is the case that the recommended way is the best, one also makes the implicit inference that among possible alternatives, this is the best one. Hence, one makes a claim to know *alternatives*. And good research that makes such constitutive claims are under the obligation to know (and sometimes also to report on) possible ways to proceed, in order to argue for the choice made. However, this claim that the way chosen is the best, is a claim about what is the case. In order to know what the case is, one needs to be oriented about possible alternatives.

So far, I hope to have made clear that in the very constitution of a research topic (no matter how descriptive it is aiming to be), there are already some important normative elements. I will follow up on this by now entering into the next – and probably more familiar - way of making a distinction between descriptive and normative statements, by looking at the conditions for validity with regard to claims about what is the case (or: fact).

Again, I take my point of departure in the simple fact that descriptions are making claims about what is the case. This, I am not going to make problematic at all – but this is not all there is to say. For how are we able to assess claims about what is the case? That is dependent on what type of sphere of validity we are talking about. Here, I will use Jürgen Habermas' distinctions. He distinguishes between the following spheres in order to show how they also imply different conditions for validity:

- The objective world, which is the totality of all that is. This sphere makes it possible to set forth claims about truth. An example: "It is raining outside today" is a claim for truth that can be decided simply by looking at what is taking place outside. Since we are, in social studies and humanities, not much interested in making claims about the physical world as such, it is not much sense in dwelling further on the conditions for validity present here. The only thing we should note, is that this type of approach to the world is one which has paradigmatic impact on our conceptions about science, to the extent that we do not understand what is really important about being human because of the prevailing impact of this paradigm. For most of us, to be human is about other things than what is possible to describe in terms of physical facts (and this is not a mere evaluative statement, it is also a claim about what is the case).
- The social world, which is the totality of legitimately regulated interpersonal relationships. This is the world in which it makes sense to set forth claims about what is normatively right. Examples like: "Genocide is prohibited and should be fought against" or "Justice is a precondition for good life in a society" receive their validity, according to Habermas, not from what we can see is a physical fact, but from the fact that people recognize these as valid statements that can direct their activities and behavior. They are nevertheless

not only normative assessments, they are statements about what is the case as well (or: What should be taken to be the case).
- The subjective world, to which the individual has privileged access, offers a basis for setting forth statements like "I believe in God" or "I love Anne". Such statements receive their validity from the fact that they are authentic statements about what is the case for the one who expresses them: Here, neither the agreement of others nor conditions in the physical world are conditions for validity – only the authenticity of the individual is.

When we deal with topics related to religion, values, and society, we first and foremost clearly address elements that have to do with the two latter spheres. Moreover, I think it is important to say that belonging to the normativity of the social world is not only normative claims like "Genocide is bad", but also more implicit statements like "The church is a community of believers". This is a statement that cannot be deducted from mere physical observations, but has to be established by means of human communication about the social sphere and how to understand it. Negotiations about how to understand both the social and the subjective world are prevailing in research, and will continue to be so, simply because the contents of these worlds are very much dependent upon how the participants understand themselves and their place in them. This fact makes the constitutive normative dimension I started out by addressing of pivotal importance. But we should also note that there all these spheres contain statements about what is the case. Hence, we have to reflect on what statements from which spheres are to be prioritized.

The distinctions between objective, normative, and subjective claims should be considered as analytic: we rarely find them in clear-cut versions. Habermas nevertheless thinks that all claims can be reconstructed as belonging to one of these types of claims. By means of such reconstruction, we can identify different means of using language and of relating to the world. Hence, communicative action as a social activity helps human relate to the world in different and meaningful ways, even when they are stating something that is not to be considered an *objective* fact (it is not meaningful simply to state that it is raining, but also that genocide is prohibited and that I believe in a just society, or in God).

In relation to the above, Habermas also stresses that the basis for validity in the social and the subjective world is human communication. Such communication is a prerequisite for developing a common framework of understanding and interpretation of these worlds. In this regard, our understanding of all the worlds (including the physical) rests on resources given in the social world, provided by the means of language.

My point is presenting Habermas here is mainly to end up by stating the following implications:

a) Even descriptive statements about the physical world rest on normative conditions.

b) Statements about society and personal life are conditioned by the regulative negotiations that allow for certain uses of language.

c) What are valid *scholarly* uses of language about the social world is dependent upon the recognition or rejection of candidates for such language in a social process. There is no objective social world, but there may be a *common*, social world.

d) Scholarly descriptions of the common social world should aim at understandings of this world that may be considered as common by all relevant participants in the scholarly community (e.g., neither internal, theological descriptions of the social world, nor descriptions of the world that neglect the impact of belief or values on how the social world is constituted).

e) Decisions about how to understand society and what to focus on is always dependent upon evaluative and normative elements; whether they are communicated / negotiated or not (in the scholarly community).

In order to get a better grasp of these points from a research point of view, we have to distance or defamiliarize ourselves from understandings of humanity or society that we easily take for granted. That is a point to which I will return in the next part of this presentation. First, let us see if we can develop some of the above further in the light of Gadamer's hermeneutics.

A few reflections based on Gadamer's hermeneutics

Gadamer's hermeneutics is basically considered to be concerned with reading texts. However, one can also read many parts of it as an attempt to develop a phenomenology of understanding, or simply as an attempt to understand what there is to understand.

Gadamer's main point is that the understanding subject is herself contributing to the process of understanding. This contribution is not a formal one, but is very much colored by the place the interpreter herself has in history. Gadamer emphasizes how we are, as humans, historical, through and through. This means that our horizon for understanding is shaped by our historical (and let me add: social and cultural) conditions.

In the process of understanding what is taking place in understanding, Gadamer distinguishes between three different elements (picking up on Heidegger), which he calls *Vorhabe, Vorsicht,* and *Vorgriff.* We may translate Vorhabe with intention, to have something in mind when approaching that which is to be interpreted. The importance here is that how this Vorhabe is shaped and given content, is determined by the historical situation of the interpreter. The world does not simply present itself to the interpreter, but the understanding is conditioned by the *Vorhabe*. Moreover, in Vorsicht is anticipated the totality of implications of the interpretation, or, the interpretation we are undertaking is grounded in something we see in advance within a wider shpere. Finally, the way we then carry out the interpretation more precisely is by the means of how we grasp the interpreted element in advance – in a Vor-griff (fore-conception) – and in a way that makes it distinct from other things we need to understand.

According to this way of understanding understanding and interpretation, the fore-structure that conditions interpretation and understanding may contain some assumptions about *how to* perceive the object of analysis / interpretation. Although these fore-elements which condition the process of understanding as such may change, they can never be left behind. This is why Gadamerian hermeneutics joins forces with Habermas in opposing a positivist approach that takes our relation to the physical world by means of the senses as the paradigm for understanding understanding. It will simply not do, if we are to understand what takes place in worlds accessible and understandable only by means of communication and language.

Finally, in this short detour on Gadamer, I would like to point out that his hermeneutics comes very close to elements in pragmatism (on which I will return later). This means that his stress on how there is always an element of application implied in understanding, may not only be valid for texts, but for other types of understanding as well. He helps us to see that the meaning of a research text is also partly constituted by the way in which we anticipate its use and function. This is, in turn, not without a normative dimension. Let us see now how this may help us further when addressing implicit and explicit normativity in research of the type we are addressing here.

On normativity in theology and religious studies

Normally, a scholar doing research in theology and or religious studies does not stand completely detached from, or neutral in regard to, her material. Her pre-conditions (both in the Gadamerian sense and other senses) and choice of study object are usually embedded in other interests, interests that might well fall "outside" the specific scope of the research in question. The guiding interests might also often be rooted in other places than in a professional competence that has already been established. Not least for theologians, guiding interests may be linked to positions in church life – at least indirectly. Hence, there are several preconditions that need to be reflected upon and addressed when conducting such research. Moreover, since research in humanities and social studies generally has some kind of normative element, according to what I have said previously, or at least has a normative horizon, it becomes even more important to bring the conditions for this research to the fore in the researcher's consciousness. The following considerations attempt to reflect on how normativity implicitly or explicitly functions in such research, and illustrate how we can become aware of this by choosing specific research strategies. Let me also say from the very outset that my remarks in the following are tacitly directed against theological research aiming solely at confirming established positions or finding new reasons for maintaining such positions. Such research is rarely able to exhibit what we celebrate as the true fruit of research: original insights and new knowledge.

An important aim of research on normativity: To defamiliarize

The basic message of this part of the lecture is the following three theses (consider how they express different types of normative claims!), which also could count as presuppositions:
- Nothing should be taken for granted in terms of how we understand human beings or the world.
- Nothing is more easily domesticized than how we understand human beings and the world.
- Research on religion (including theology), values, and society should *alienate* us from the life-world in which these exist, in order to see what we take for granted and what the alternatives to the contents of this life-world are.

As a result of practicing these recommendations, we will be able to better understand implicit and explicit normativity when we understand humans, human society, and religiously founded worldviews. I will try to make clear the relevance of these theses by using some examples from recent contributions to research on contemporary religion.

The importance of these presuppositions can be realized when we look at what are the most important functions of a religiously shaped view of world and self: it is to provide individuals and groups with resources or means for shaping, developing, and sustaining identities. Because we speak of identities, we speak of something very close to us, something hard to get a good understanding of without being confronted with something else, something else that can be disturbing, puzzling. The identity-position of a person or a group and its inherent normativity thus becomes conscious when one becomes aware of its inevident character, which may emerge from the confrontation with what is different, or alternative. Exactly because religion and theology have such a tremendous impact on the formation of people's (often also including the researcher's) life-world and values, it is important to establish a reflexive distance to this life-world.

The basic assumption, on which my three theses are made, is that there is a strong degree of normativity in the given understandings of the human / human society and religiously founded worldviews. That should not be surprising to anyone. But what does it mean when we talk about their implicit or explicit normative character? Without any presumptions of being exhaustive, I will suggest the following:

- Implicit normativity is that which functions tacitly, it is not verbalized or thematized, and serves as a "taken-for-granted" assumptions about the matters in question.
- Explicit normativity expresses itself in the normative elements that are used as formative, disciplinary, and evaluative. It is taken as part of the easily accessible reservoir of articulated assumptions of what the human being and / or the world is / should be.

There can be an overlap between explicit and implicit normativity, but such an overlap is not necessary: often there are implicit norms or normative elements that are never explicitly articulated in research (and in the research's object of analysis), but which nevertheless functions as formative patters for the ways more explicit norms are developed or articulated.

In order to explain how this link between implicit and explicit normativity works and can be brought to awareness, we can use a common example from Christian ethics: either this ethics is understood along communitarian lines, as ethics for Christians and / or the Christian community. Or Christian ethics is just another way of expressing the ethics that is common to all humans, what is good for all and can be realized by all people of good will as the best way of living. These two patterns, usually or commonly labeled as communitarianism or universalism, respectively, shape the form, content and understanding of what ethics is like, often without being sufficiently explicated themselves. Hence, it is not always explicit to what extent these patterns of order are functioning as normative, and it might very well be that such patterns may exist in both material to be researched or in the researcher herself, without being called to attention. I would suggest that elements like those identified by the communitarianism / universalism dichotomy serve as important implicit elements in many contemporary religiously founded worldviews. We will return to this point in a little while.

Before I proceed with another example, let me just make one remark on the notion of *normativity*. Normativity is problematic when it precludes us of from seeing what we should be able to see as researchers. In the game of investigating the familiar, it is easy to get blind because of internalized normativities. I have already mentioned that this might be because of the position one might have in church life, but it can also be because of gender, because of what one perceives to be politically correct, etc. Hence, we need different theoretical approaches that can defamiliarize what we see, in order to see other things and more. This is an important and rather basic argument for *theoretical pluralism*: such pluralism can destabilize established ways of reading o understanding by challenging them, and thereby also offering them a new awareness that offers chances for explicating their hitherto implicit reasons.

How implicit normativity is at work in different views of the human, including theological anthropology, is well illustrated by the recent work of Swedish ethicist Staffan Nilsson.[1] He has done research on different theological, philosophical, and other ways of understanding human self-actualization. The study is theological, but may also be of interest for pedagogy and psychology. In his study, Nilsson makes quite a few interesting observations about these different understandings. In the end he manag-

---

1 S. Nilsson: *Den potentiella Människan. En undersökning av teorier om självförverkligande*. Doctoral dissertation, Uppsala 2005.

es to make a basic distinction between two ways of understanding self-actualization, based on two clearly distinguishable and separable understandings of what it is to be human: These understandings he calls *relational*, resp., *internalist* models of self-actualization.

The relational approach underscores how human self-fulfillment has to take place in a life shared with others, and with access to common resources of society and culture, while the internalist approach sees the human's quest for self-fulfillment as a process in which he / she develops intrinsic capacities, etc. These underlying patterns thus shape not only how one understands different ways humans live, but also what to look for, how one evaluates different practices, and in general: the total optic within which one understands and relates to human life. Hence the basic patterns might remain implicit, but still serve to shape the understanding of both explicitly normative elements as well as the understanding of what is important.

One of the points Nilsson makes, is worth commenting on from a more theoretical point of view. Nilsson asserts that he would not have been able to make the distinctions he makes, nor separate out these different patterns, unless he had been making a *comparative* study. Comparative studies have the advantage of making clear alternatives to the given and present normativity, and they thereby serve to defamiliarize more easily or readily the patterns that underlie and shape the material – or the researcher's preconditions for the understanding of the material.[2] This is even more vividly illustrated if we go to a recent contribution to empirical research of religion:

In the research of Paul Heelas and Linda Woodhead at Lancaster University, e.g. in their book *Religion in modern times* (2000), they present – in my opinion successfully – a typology that helps clarify the patterns that may shape normative elements. Their typology of religions helps to make explicit what is often taken for granted and working as implicit factors shaping how different types of religion (and religious societies) are configured:

- *Religions of difference*, which are based on the distinction between God and Humans, Christian and not-Christian, active and passive

---

2 The Norwegian anthropologist T. Hylland-Eriksen speaks of "the blindness at home" which it is necessary to overcome. Hence, the study of the foreign is about making it less foreign, and about making the familiar less so. See his *Small places, large issues: an introduction to social and cultural anthropology*, London: Pluto Press 2001.

Christians, women and men, lay and clergy, sinners and saints, etc. In these forms of religion, authority (and thereby also normativity) is mainly shaped, sustained and expressed by emphasis on such differences. Any attempt to destabilize these differences is met with skepticism or rejection, of which the changing of gender roles or the present controversial issue of homosexuality is among the best illustrations. An important component in this type of religion is that religious authority is externally based, and that humans have to be obedient to this, even when this authority appears to be in conflict with personal interests or convictions.

Through this description, Heelas and Woodhead establish a perspective on the explicit normativity of views concerning humans and the world which contributes to disclosing the underlying, implicit patterns of these. This disclosure is also present in their description of what they call

- *Religions of Humanity*. In contrast to *Religions of difference*, this mode of shaping the normative patterns of religion is aimed at building down differences and emphasis on what is common to all. Here the main point is not to stress that humans are sinners and God is holy, but that humans are created in the image of God, and that all are loved by God without exception. The normative elements in this type of religion are explicitly oriented towards love for the neighbor, and how all humans take part in the same community. Religions are here seen as expressions of human experience, not as based upon a revelation external to human grasp or control (which would be the case in the previous type). Often, a more positive, "optimistic" or affirmative anthropology is expressed here.[3] This optimism also expresses itself in a more harmonious configuration of religious authority: although religious authority is still seen as externally based, it is in principle in accordance with human experience.

As we see, both these types of religion and religiously based normativity place the authority outside the human: What obliges the human to do this or that, is God or the other in need. As Heelas and Woodhead write in

---

3 For the sake of fairness, it has to be added that Heelas and Woodhead differentiate the analytic categories presented here further, into experiential religions of difference, resp. religions of humanity. It can be discussed to what extent their categories also express their own normativity, but the main point here is to stress how their categories emerge out of empirically based work, and make the researcher able to see implicit configurations of normativity that are usually not explicitly stated by the adherents themselves.

a more recent book, these types represent "'Life-as' forms of the sacred, which emphasize a transcendent source of significance and authority to which individuals must conform" (*The Spiritual Revolution,* 2005, 6.)

One of their actual criticisms of these types of religion is that the conformity they demand seems to take place at the expense of the cultivation of humans' personal experience of themselves, so that not all experiences, feelings of subjective states are recognized as valid. This is one of the reasons why they think organized traditional religion today seems to be declining. What is growing, on the other hand, is what they call

- *Spiritualities of life.* These describe the implicit normative elements in types of anthropology and worldviews such as "Subjective-life forms of the sacred, which emphasize inner sources of significance and authority and the cultivation or sacralization of unique subjective-lives" and claim that these "are most likely to be growing in the foreseeable future" (cf. Heelas and Woodhead 2005: 6).

Heelas' and Woodhead's description could, I think, be easily utilized by anyone doing research in the field of religion and theology. Their typology challenges the researcher to ask *explicitly:*

- What kind of understanding of theology / anthropology / the world is explicit and / or implicit in the material I am researching?
- What kind of understanding of Christianity is implicitly present as part of my own pre-conceptions of the material and or my own understanding of what Christianity is like?

By this way of formulating the questions, it should be clear that the questions about implicit and explicit normativity have to go both ways: both directed towards the material, and towards the researcher herself. Hence, the application of models and theories developed in other contexts may very well serve as an adequate tool for letting awareness of implicit normativities emerge.

Allow me to make a personal and self-critical note: I think the above suggestions are indicating some of the things which we could have done a better job on when presenting our own basis for assessing the empirical material in *Gud på Sørlandet.* This study was a qualitative research project that looked into changing patterns of religion in the southern part of Norway (the bible-belt) (See Henriksen & Repstad 2005 and Repstad and Henriksen [Eds] 2005). As one may guess, the books from the project received some critical attention, especially from the "religious establishment", but also from others, who claimed that we had a hidden theological agenda. I see no problem with the fact that we in the study developed an analysis that was based on what may also be interpreted as a normative theoretical framework [Woodhead and Heelas], or our own theological preferences. Nevertheless, we should have made far more explicit what we did and why we made the assessments we made when we commented upon some features of religious life that we disclosed in our analyses. It would probably have altered the balance between a more descriptive presentation of the empirical material, and a more explanatory and theological dimension in the book. Despite the fact that this would have required more detailed arguments, it may have been worth it – also because our opponents and critics would then have had to relate to and establish alternatives to the normative claims that we should have been basing our assessments on, instead of just referring to them as matters of personal opinion or our already established theological points of view).

I have used the three examples of categorization in order to make visible the interplay between implicit and explicit normativity. Although the examples differ: two from moral philosophy and one from religious studies, they all illustrate such interplay. At the same time, normativity is also linked to formal or informal authority. This has just been hinted at, but in my conclusion I will return to the question about how to establish authoritative positions that can be accepted as authoritative.

Another implicit normativity: how to relate to the past

From a theological point of view, perhaps the strongest challenge Heelas and Woodhead present relates to how Christianity is rooted in an historical past. This past is, needless to say, not something that is subjectively based, and there is in it a kind of authoritative framework to which anyone has to relate to be part of the Christian tradition. This past, however, can only make sense to contemporary people if it is, as Kierkegaard would say, *subjectively appropriated*. One of the implicit normative elements in much of theology is in what this appropriation consists of. To put it in a formula, we could say that either:

- I appropriate the (understanding of the) past by trying to live and shape my life according to the patterns that can be found there, so that my experiences shall/ought to make sense in relation to a given past. This is what happens when conservative Christians try to live like they did in the first Christian communities. (This is a way of using the past as a pattern for conformity and discipline).

- Another, alternative approach would be to ask to what extent and in what manner the understanding of the past can help us to interpret the present, and provide us with resources for understanding the challenges we find ourselves confronted with. Then the past would not serve as a given pattern to which we have to conform and discipline ourselves, but would be the reservoir of modes of understanding with the potential to help expand our understanding of the present situation. (This is a way of understanding the past as a resource for understanding dimensions of the present).

This way of spelling out the alternatives is perhaps a too clear-cut way of understanding the implicit function of the past, but it nevertheless serves to identify something which in turn shapes a lot of explicitly expressed normative expectations, especially in religious communities, which are also sometimes present when secular people turn to religious traditions to find answers to complicated postmodern dilemmas. The first mode will always offer an a priori authoritative status to the past, and thereby demand some kind of discipline in the adherents of the tradition rooted in this past. What it ignores, is that the past does not necessarily represent our present conditions of life. Hence, the lack of consonance between past and present implies that there will always be an unending process of negotiations, adjustments and accommodations in order to make sense not only of the past accepted, but also of why one does not fully accept the past.

The second mode is more oriented towards integrating the resources of the past with present conditions, not neglecting the past as important to our present conditions of life, but nevertheless realizing that we know more, might have a wider understanding of issues etc., than what was given in the past. Hence, the need to explain why we do not take over everything from the past or feel obliged to discipline ourselves solely to patterns of the past, disappears. It does not mean an arbitrary approach to past elements of tradition, but a responsible one, in which one takes into consideration reasons for why one relates to the past and present in the way one does, and *articulates* these reasons.

I think it is possible to detect tendencies in recent religion where both these patterns are at work. Partly, we see it in the theological discussion between *foundationalism* and *coherentism*: foundationalism, which expresses and articulates the basis (in the past) on which all belief must build, and coherentism, which stresses how we have to integrate the knowledge of past and present into a coherent whole where this knowledge also make a place for our beliefs.[4] A coherentist approach is one in which we constantly have to articulate regulating normativity and ask for its implications and relation to other elements of knowledge. This is not the same case in a foundationalist approach, however, which more easily assumes basic normativity as the starting point for ongoing reflections. A foundationalist approach can in this context be seen as one where the past is the foundation for the present, while in a coherentist approach the task is to facilitate a constant process of integration between past and present – which is not the same thing.

(Note here also how fundationalism may be seen as being in accordance with the positivist and non-hermeneutical paradigm that sees science as based on the paragim of the physical world, while the coherentist approach may be seen as in accordance with Gadamer's and Habermas' emphasis on the always to be negotiated basis for understanding the social and historical world in which we find ourselves).

Moreover, the distinction between different modes of relating to the past transcends these distinctions and discussions, which are often located in systematic theology, and extends into relations between different theological disciplines: One can occasionally find exegetes and historians who seem to think that once the approach of the past to a certain question is clarified, the issues in question are solved. This seems to be the tacit or implicit normative position of some exegetes in the present discussion in many churches on homosexuality: if we know what Paul meant and wrote in the past and why, we know what to mean and to do in the present. Others will say that this is no longer relevant for us, as we are in a quite different historical situation, have other types of knowledge and institutions, and so on. In any case, we here find implicit assumptions about both human beings and religious views of the world. Of course, which stand one chooses to take here will also be related to normative decisions – and to how one understands the relation between religion and empirical knowledge. Perhaps we can formulate the question like this: Should we understand the relation between past and present as a possible competition or as a possibility for expanding coherent knowledge in order to make more solid and well-based normative decisions?

---

4   On this discussion, see e.g. W. van Huyssteen: *The Shaping of Rationality: Toward Interdisciplinarity in Theology and Science,* Grand Rapids: Eerdmans 1999.

A normative conclusion

As a kind of open conclusion, we can say that while the results of religious reflection aim at articulating a normativity that must be in accordance with the canon of holy texts, these results cannot be understood as *deduced* from such texts alone. This is true both of reflections that relate to the Bible as well as to the Qur'an. I believe one of the tasks for us as scholars of religion and theology is to make this visible, in order to bring to the fore that normative matters with regard to religion are not so easily understood as is sometimes assumed by the public. Sheila Davaney very aptly illustrates this in the following quote:

> It is also the nature of human interpretation and appropriation that makes mere repetition impossible. Humans engage the canons, the broad inheritance of their tradition, from particular locales for particular purposes and these shape what is engaged, highlighted, criticized, and even being discerned as being present in tradition at all. *All appropriation of tradition entails, therefore, its creative transformation into something new that then becomes a part of that inheritance"* [5] (italics by J-O.H.).

The discussions of normativity within theology and religious studies are very different from each other. In theology, it can probably not be separated from the critical understanding of how the Bible is understood *and used* as a normative source of life and doctrine in the Church.[6] Hence how Scriptural authority is to be affirmed is in itself a systematic and normative question, and cannot be treated as isolated from the discussion of other systematic issues.[7] To establish normativity is, consequently, a *communicative, communitarian and hermeneutical* enterprise. In order to

---

5   Davaney, *Pragmatic Historicism*, 107.
6   However, this does not say anything about how the Bible should be used, and that is where the task truly lies for anyone who is interested in the normative status of the Bible. I agree with C. H. Cosgrove, who in *Appealing to Scripture in Moral debate: Five Hermeneutical Rules,* indicates that it is the purpose of the rule rather than the rule itself which has to be given most weight in moral reasoning (12f.). This way of thinking is also illuminating for the hermeneutical task of systematic theology in general: it can only be done properly as long as we differentiate between the basis, the concern and the actual expression given with a certain position.
7   This is e.g., realized by W. Pannenberg in his treatment of Scripture in *Systematische Theologie*, Vandenhoeck & Ruprecht 1989-1993.

validate what should count as normative, we have to take into account reasons based on history, experience, science, tradition, and society as well as Scripture. The hermeneutical task of establishing transparent normativity is linked to the *negotiation* of all those reasons in relation to each other. Hence, normativity and rationality in theological discourse presuppose and justify each other reciprocally. There can be no normativity without communicable reasons that can be discussed (and thereby, implicitly: understood). And there can be no meaningful discussion of reasons without the assumption that they are recognized as potentially normative. As a consequence of the interplay between normativity and rationality a justified claim for *authority* arises. This claim presupposes the recognition of the possible *truth* in the position developed. In this sense, to make explicit the implicit normative content of theology should be seen as a contributor to a rational as well as a normative enterprise. The normative content of worldviews and understandings of humankind cannot, and does not, in the long run exist separately from their rationality. Normative claims, can therefore not be seen as constituted of other elements than the reasons emerging for a discourse saturated by historicity, embedded in, and part of, history.[8]

Rationality is constituted by someone offering reasons that others (but not necessarily everyone) can have the possibility to give their consent to. The recognition of a reason as worthy of consent implies the recognition of its normativity. Such reasons are given in and by the voices of the past, through experience, history, and thinking. This shows the importance and relevance of taking *any possible reason* into account when establishing a position, in order to try to make this position as coherent as possible. Thus the different elements and reasons can mutually support each other, restrict each other's implications, and thereby contribute to a more precise (but never final) result.

The dimension of normativity in fields such as the ones we are dealing with here, consequently appears through the ability to suggest well-informed and well-grounded approaches to research problems, based on (or rather: worked out from) a description that takes the above stated conditions for rationality into account.

---

8   Cf. also Davaney, op. cit, 114, who emphasises how this also implies that there can be no turning away from the past or that it should be ignored. However, she also point here to how we have to realise that our conception of the past is marked by us, is our construction.

Thus, to articulate the implicit and explicit normativity in interpretations of human society and its values, and religious worldviews, as well as criticizing them, implies the necessary historicizing of all types of statements that are hermeneutically based and related to a continuous negotiation as to how to be articulated. This historicizing process does not exclude the normativity of theology, but it implies that the reasons behind the statements formulated constantly have to be scrutinized and appropriated anew.[9] This goes for all the actual formulations of normative positions and interpretations as well.[10]

References

Albinus, Lars, Armin W. Geertz, and Peter Widmann: (Eds.): *Værdier i religionsforskning og religionsundervisning i Danmark*. Århus: Det Teologiske fakultet, Århus universitet, 2001.

Cosgrove, Charles H.: *Appealing to Scripture in Moral Debate: Five Hermeneutical Rules*. Grand Rapids: Eerdmans 2002.

Davaney, Sheila Greeve. *Pragmatic Historicism: A Theology for the Twenty-First Century*. Albany, N.Y.: State University of New York Press, 2000.

Gadamer, Hans Georg. *Truth and Method*. 2nd, rev. ed. New York: Crossroad, 1989.

Habermas, Jürgen: *Nachmetaphysisches Denken*. Frankfurt: Suhrkamp 1986.

Heelas, Paul, and Woodhead, Linda: *The Spiritual Revolution*. Oxford: Blackwell 2005.

Henriksen, Jan-Olav: "Researching Theological Normativity: Some Critical and Constructive Suggestions." *Studia Theologica 60*, no. 2 (2006): 207-20.

Henriksen, Jan-Olav, and Repstad, Pål: *Tro i sør. Sosiologiske og teologiske blikk på sørlandsk religion*. Bergen: Fagbokforlaget 2006.

---

9   To use the words of LeRon Shults, when he formulates the task of postfoundationalist theology: it consists in "to engage in an interdisciplinary dialogue within our postmodern culture while both maintaining a commitment to intersubjective, transcommunal theological argumentation for the truth of Christian faith, and recognizing the provisionality of our historical embedded understandings and culturally conditioned explanations of the Christian tradition and religious experience." *The Postfoundationalist Task of Theology*, Eerdmans 1999, 237. Cf. also W. van Huyssteen: The Shaping of Rationality: Toward Interdisciplinarity in Theology and Science, Eerdmans 1999, 243.

10 Cf. again Davaney, op. cit., 88: "The interpretations that come forth from this process will be human products, fallible and fragile attempts to name reality, what is most ultimate within it, and how humans should live life today in the face of the final mystery and unknowing that pervades all historical existence." Also ibid., 150: "Our normative imaginations and judgments, as all other dimensions of human life, are traditioned."

Hylland-Eriksen, Thomas: *Small places, large issues: an introduction to social and cultural anthropology*, London: Pluto Press 2001.

Kuhn, Thomas Samuel. *The Structure of Scientific Revolutions*. Chicago: University of Chicago Press, 1970.

Nilsson, Staffan: *Den potentiella Människan. En undersökning av teorier om självförverkligande*. Doctoral dissertation, Uppsala University 2005.

Pannenberg, Wolfhart: *Systematische Theologie Band 1-3*, Göttingen: Vandenhoeck & Ruprecht 1989-1993.

Repstad, Pål, and Henriksen, Jan-Olav: *Mykere kristendom? Sørlandsreligion i endring* Bergen: Fagbokforlaget 2005.

Shults, F. LeRon: *The Postfoundationalist Task of Theology*, Eerdmans 1999,

Storstein Haug, Kari: "Cultural Empirical Studies and Normativity: A Case from Missiology" in this volume.

van Huyssteen, J. Wentzel: *The Shaping of Rationality: Toward Interdisciplinarity in Theology and Science*, Grand Rapids: Eerdmans 1999.

Woodhead, Linda and Heelas, Paul: *Religion in modern Times. An interpretative Anthology*. Oxford: Blackwell, 2000.

Empirical research and theological normativity

Ulla Schmidt

Normativity and theology

Normativity pervades our lives, the British philosopher Onora O'Neill claims (Korsgaard, 1996: xi). We regularly encounter claims to the effect that we ought to do certain actions, be in certain ways, or believe certain things. Formally, normativity can be defined as a property by virtue of which a proposition or set of propositions recommend or demand that something is being done or abstained from, praised or blamed, believed or denied, pursued or rejected. In this sense normativity entails guidance of human action, character and beliefs. This leads to the question whether or not we are thereby actually bound to act, be or believe in that way. In other words, a normative claim involves the question whether or not that particular claim is justified and legitimate, and merits our approval and compliance. Normativity is therefore closely related to a set of neighboring issues such as justification, reasoning, legitimacy and authority.

Questions about the conditions on which such normative recommendations or demands to be, believe or act in certain ways can be considered plausible, valid or true, are systematically dealt with in disciplines such as theology, ethics and epistemology. Epistemology includes the question on which conditions demands to accept or reject certain beliefs about reality are valid, ethics investigates the condition for accepting or rejecting actions, virtues or values as commendable and praiseworthy, and theology examines the condition on which claims regarding reality, human life and its relation to God are valid and plausible. Within Christian religion we find propositions and statements such as "Jesus Christ is the Son of God and our savior", or "Love thy neighbor!", implying a claim to acquiesce in these statements. Christian theology does not simply reiterate such statements, but discusses the conditions on which they might be true or valid. It raises the question whether or not they are justified in terms of there being sufficient reasons to adopt them. A moral tradition or common moral sense might entail claims such as "compassion is a virtue which ought to be developed, nurtured and practiced", or "it is wrong to deceive others by intention". Ethics, be it as a theological or philosophical discipline, investigates and discusses critically the conditions on which such claims might or might not be valid or true.

Normative claims to a large extent have the hold they have on us as a result of upbringing and socialization. They are effective because we have grown accustomed to them, not necessarily because we have explicitly examined and accepted them. In this sense we might speak about "tacit" or "implicit" normativity (Henriksen, 2006). Obviously this form of implicit normativity should not be confused with just any kind of social, economic or other force which affects and influences human behavior and conduct. What characterizes normativity, tacit or explicit, in distinction to economic forces or social structures which also shape human behavior and conduct, is that normativity shapes human conduct and belief by conveying the idea that some beliefs and forms of conduct are good, right, truthful, laudable, rational, etc. An important dimension of disciplines such as theology or ethics is therefore that they uncover tacit normativities and enable us to take a step back from their self-evident grip in order to examine them critically. In this sense we might distinguish between unexamined and examined normativity. It goes without saying that the tacit, unexamined normative claims might be at odds with the explicit and examined normative claims. The explicit teaching in a Christian congregation might be to welcome people from all socio-economic strata of society, but its actual practices might tacitly signal that only those from a particular social background or people with a certain level of functioning are actually welcome.

At a formal level normative propositions can be of a first and second order. Whereas religion or moral traditions make first order normative statements, theology and ethics as critical reflection entail normative statements of a second order. This resembles what Ganzevoort in adherence to George Lindbeck labels first and second order theological discourse (Ganzevoort, 2005: 20–21). However, although this formal distinction might be useful as an analytical tool when approaching the field, many positions will argue that the theoretical reflection within theology and ethics can not be entirely separated from the actually lived tradition of morality and Christian religion, but is quite on the contrary intertwined with it.

This indicates that closely entwined with the issue of normativity is the question about the validity of normative claims. This, in its turn, evokes the question about which reasons provide evidence of the validity of such claims in a justificatory process. What could be relevant reasons in the reflective process of examining and determining valid normative claims?

This article explores one particular candidate for such reasons in theological normative reflection, namely knowledge produced through empirical research within social sciences. Could insights generated through empirical research provide evidence of the validity of normative claims? The article will start by laying out the background for this question, before discussing whether or not it is feasible to consider ordinary beliefs as significant to normative reflection within theology, concentrating especially on the epistemological dimensions of this question. At the end it explores concrete examples of empirical research and examines their potential normative significance. I will argue that whereas the traditional objections from epistemology and ethics do not preclude ordinary beliefs from normative reflection, the methodological difficulties seem to be considerable. It should be noted from the outset that theology and theological reflection is here confined to a Christian religious tradition.

Theology, as critical reflection on the conditions of validity of propositions and statements within Christian religion, relates to normativity in two ways. First, Christian religion has a cognitive dimension of doctrine where certain beliefs about reality, human beings, and their relation to a transcendent God, are claimed to be true, and therefore to be acknowledged and accepted. But these propositions are typically understood to be more than a cognitive description of reality. They also lay claim on the believer and require that he or she trusts them. They claim to have implications for the forming of human life and of a Christian community, the church. Thus they are not only doctrines and teachings about reality and its alleged relation to God, but also about valid, good and right forms of individual and collective life (Andersen et al., 2002: 96–97). Unlike dominant strands of enlightenment and modern traditions of ethics where the notion of right conduct and actions has been broken off from a larger account of reality, separating the good from real, normative propositions within theology do not necessarily disconnect belief about reality from claims related to human conduct, character and practical life.

Theological normativity and empirical research: traditional assumptions, criticisms and new approaches

The question of this article is partly motivated by a traditional assumption that normativity and empirical research constitute a duality and ought to be kept separate. This assumption has gained support from the side of empirical research as well as from the side of those concerned with normative disciplines. Max Weber famously argued for what he called value-freedom in sociological and economic sciences, implying that they lacked basis for and should abstain from "value-judgments", which he defined as "practical judgments of phenomena within our control, as either reprehensible or favorable" (Weber, 1999: 108). That would also include evaluation of certain religious traditions and religious social forms. Committed to purposes such as attaining knowledge and truth, and questioning unexamined features and conditions of human life, Weber notices how science is obviously not free of values altogether. It contains normativity in the sense that it values truth over deception, more insight over less, and methodological transparency over pure intuition. Furthermore, empirical sciences can indeed research value assessments and their historical, psychological or individual conditions, providing among other things a better understanding of competing values in society as well as of atypical value positions. But no particular imperative or normative ethics follow from or can be advocated on the basis of this kind of empirical research (Weber, 1999: 118).

Growing acknowledgement of the extent to which science not only incorporates values associated with its inherent goods and regulative principles, but are driven by interests and goals, has for a long time challenged the idea that science can avoid tacitly or openly recommending or condemning some values over others. Much attention has been devoted to the way empirical research is tacitly normatively freighted, not the least through social constructivism, and various forms of feminist, postmodern and post-colonial theory of sciences. And methods such as some forms of evaluation research and action research have made it an explicit goal for research to assist development and improvement of programs. The view that empirical research cannot be kept free of normative evaluations of social practices has thus become commonplace.

Parallel criticisms against mixing normativity and empirical research have been presented from the side of normatively oriented disciplines, such as theology and ethics. In general, normative disciplines' criticisms against ascribing normative significance to empirical research have derived from a main idea that normative claims can be legitimately compelling for human conduct, only if they are themselves not subject to the historical contingencies of human conduct. Normativity must be elevated above the historically contingent, based on something not itself exposed to and manageable by human will, choice and action. This kind of foundation for normativity beyond the historically contingent has been differently defined. Within ethics, some theories have grounded binding ethical obligations and ideals in natural law. Others have developed them on the basis of a universal reason, in terms of universal principles and obligations. In theology, other theories have in similar ways defined a basis of true and valid theological, normative propositions allegedly independent of historically contingent aspects and human conditions. The kerygmatic and dialectical theology in the first half of the 20th century emphasized God's revelation in Christ, entirely different from all there is and untainted by and independent of human history, as the ground of theological statements and insight. Biblicist inspired approaches have underlined God's revelation as it is deposited and contained in the Bible as the basis for theological statements, arguing that normative propositions are warranted as valid by being convincing explications of biblical content. If normativity is based on the historical processes of human action, it basically becomes subject to human mastery and control, and thus incapable of binding human conduct. It reduces theological propositions about God to expressions of human practice and understanding. Proponents of such theories rarely deny that theological normative propositions have in fact changed and thus are in fact affected by history and human practices. But that, so the argument typically goes, does not conflict with the idea that such claims can be firmly based on sources not themselves exposed to contingent change, it simply implies that we can be better at detecting what these sources truly tell us. Historical changes to the content of normativities are a token of growing insight into the sources, such as the Bible, rather than an indication that the idea of ahistoric normativity is flawed in the first place. That is not to say that these kinds of theories have not paid any attention to empirical research. But to the extent that they have, empirical research has been considered instrumental and subordinate to normative reflection. Empirical research has at best played an ancillary role, assisting implementation of normative instructions in relation to human belief and conduct, but insignificant in determining or informing normative content and normative propositions.

Just like the view that empirical research is free of normative and evaluative claims has been challenged, so has the understanding that normativity must be fenced off from empirical observations and research. Contextual theologies, such as liberation theology, have asserted that normative propositions cannot be defined and validated independently of the social, cultural and historical context in which theology is immersed and done. Ecclesial theologies, exemplified by Stanley Hauerwas, have focused on how theological, normative propositions are validated in relation to the context of a community of faith, formed by and gathered around practices, values and ideals. Each represents approaches where empirical facts about a given context would be relevant to the determination of normative content. Nonetheless, even within these kinds of theological approaches, empirical research has rarely been used to provide a more systematic inclusion and consideration of knowledge and insight concerning actual practices and contexts.

What this account of separation and criticisms against separation between normativity and empirical research shows, is that the relation between normativity and empirical research cannot be determined in general without specifying what is meant by each respectively (Schweitzer, 2005: 88). It can only be determined with respect to particular accounts of normativity and empirical research. Three accounts raise the question about potential normative significance of empirical research of social phenomena in ways that help formulating and specifying relevant questions to the issue and therefore deserve closer consideration.

In a fairly recent article, Thomas Lewis discusses how ethnographic research should inform normative reflection on ethical questions within comparative religious ethics. Lewis alludes to well-known developments in ethical theory, from an emphasis on principles delivered by a universal morality, to a concern with the many ways morality unfolds in human life, especially processes of moral formation. This anthropological turn in ethics not only invites more "fine-grained accounts of the human subject", but also suggests that more attention is paid to everyday life and the different practices through which moral character is cultivated (2010: 398). Furthermore, Lewis acknowledges how detailed ethnographic studies of a particular context and setting might prevent hasty references to religious traditions' ethics and morality in uniform rather than plural terms, in the general rather than in the local. Nonetheless, he questions whether there is sufficient support for allowing this kind of research to inform normative reflection. It might provide a rich and varied description of moral life and how it is learned, lived and transmitted. But the mere fact that people live and act in a particular way does not in and of itself offer a reason why others ought to live and act that way as well, he states. That would require an additional argument, one which empirical research is unable to provide. Lewis is especially concerned with how attempts at deriving relevant information for normative reflection from these insights is at risk of simply reproducing the researcher's own pre-reflective beliefs and views (Lewis, 2010: 400). Not only does this, as is commonly acknowledged, call for the researcher's reflection on her own position, it also points in the direction of a further question about the justification of why this position should be approved. Thus, Lewis seems prone to think that so far, no satisfying argument has been provided for allowing empirical research, such as ethnography, to influence normative reflection.

Jaco Dreyer asks how normativity, which always recommends that certain phenomena in the world, such as beliefs, actions, what we value in life, political institutions, etc. ought or ought not to be in a certain way, can be linked to context. He refers to Paul Ricoeur's notion of imagination as a viable approach, where imagination is placed in a tension between on the one hand utopia and on the other ideology, between critique and conservation. Applied to the question regarding normativity and how to link it to context, Dreyer asserts that theological and religious normativities need innovation in order not to turn into negative ideologizing and distortion, but on the other hand also need connection with tradition in order not to lose its connection with praxis (2005: 7). His claim is that empirical research can contribute fruitfully to balancing these two sides. On one hand it might provide insights into the dimension of imagination related to ideology, by highlighting self-understanding, practices and social characteristics of religious communities and religious believers. Thereby it might prevent normativities from losing contact with reality. On the other hand, it can open up new possibilities by highlighting innovations and criticisms of normativities deposited in traditions. This requires, however, that empirical research and the empirical researcher comply with principles of what he calls critical hermeneutics, which moves within the well-known dialectical span between distanciation and belonging (2005: 13).

A third account envisaging and discussing a potential, normative significance of empirical studies in religion and theology is offered by Jeff Astley, in terms of what he calls a "plea for the study of ordinary theology" (2002). Starting from an understanding of learning as any enduring change brought about by experience as "we learn our values, dispositions, attitudes, feelings and skills as well as in our beliefs and understanding" (2002: 4), he underscores how learning is significant for religion and its learning context is important for our theology. In his view, one of the main products of learning within this context of religion is what he calls ordinary theology, which he defines as "the theology and theologizing of Christians who have received little or no theological education of a scholarly, academic or systematic kind" (2002: 56). It is not primarily related to the beliefs and believing of common religion, but mainly refers to churchgoers. Using the notion of theology in this context of the ordinary presupposes, Astley admits, a broadened definition of the activity and phenomenon of theology to comprise reflective speaking and discourse about God or the divine or what we worship. It is not restricted to the systematic and disciplined activities covered by academic theology. Religious beliefs should not be called theology unless they involve some degree of articulation and reflection. But, Astley asserts, most believers do engage in some measure of reflection and articulation regarding their beliefs, they address the intellectual challenges that faith engenders. Ordinary believers can in fact be expected to be "committed to normative self-criticism of their faith, including a critical dialogue with Christian sources and some reflection on practical situations and their own actions within them" (2002: 142). Ordinary theology thus understood is clearly accessible to empirical studies in terms of a range of social scientific tools: qualitative, ethnographic research as well as quantitative research such as survey-data (2002: 97–98). Studies of ordinary theology are theologically relevant, and might contribute to theology in its more specialized sense, including the discussion of theological normative propositions. Here he leans on David Hudson's view of rationality and criteria for rational beliefs, where one such criterion is conformity to a rational system of beliefs, by which he means a system widely held to be rational and regulative of our talk and action (Astley, 2002: 154–158). A relevant parallel to other normative systems defines conformity to a system of beliefs held widely and consistently by a group of people within a context of Christianity, as a relevant criterion of orthodoxy, together with other formal criteria such as conformity with Scripture and tradition. Acceptance and appraisal of a belief within a group of "ordinary, faithful, practicing Christians", cannot be irrelevant to a belief's status within church doctrine, a point alluded to by the catholic notion of the "consensus of the faithful" (2002: 159).

These accounts all discuss the possibility of assigning normative significance to insights derived from empirical research, each offering points to the discussion that are worthy of consideration and will help bring out and articulate some of the pressing question in this connection.

Theological, normative reflection: Could it be informed by empirical research?

According to the description above, theology critically discusses and examines whether and how normative propositions regarding beliefs and conduct can be warranted as valid. It entails a process of justification where reasons are invoked as evidence for the validity of such claims and propositions. This process of reasoning and justification is obviously a continuous, open-ended process, where conclusions are always in principle provisional. Different theological approaches will have different views of what could count as relevant reasons. References to Scripture, history and tradition of churches, human experience, scientific insights and principles of rationality typically tend to be considered, although different theological approaches might evaluate their merit and relevance differently. The question to be discussed here is whether actual religious life with its beliefs and conduct might also be a reason providing evidence of validity of normative claims. Is it relevant to the question about how to legitimately formulate belief in God within Christian theology, what people actually do believe about God in a Christian context? Do actually held moral beliefs regarding same sex relations, euthanasia, or how to relate properly to authorities in a Christian community have any bearing on what could legitimately be claimed by theological reflection as a valid and binding proposition? This is not on a par with the question whether such beliefs do in fact influence theological formulations of valid, normative propositions, which they obviously do, given theology's social embeddedness. It is a question about warranting such propositions in the course of critical reflection by inferring as a reason the fact that certain things are believed and others not.

The obvious objection would be that theology's task is precisely the opposite, to bracket and question those beliefs and examine whether or not there are good reasons for them, apart from the fact that they are being held. This resembles the question raised by Thomas Lewis, namely that the fact that people act in a certain way, does not in itself constitute a reason why others ought to follow suit. That someone holds a belief, is not in and of itself a reason why others ought to do likewise, so this objection would go. This view, however, seems to presuppose a particular understanding of what a religious belief is, an understanding that precludes reflection or probing of reasons from such beliefs, defining it as the proper task and privilege of specialized, trained theologians. Clearly, religious, Christian beliefs concerning such things as God's being and nature, the goods of human life, the fundamental nature of being and the character of a potential, renewed human community, are complex and composite phenomena. They are influenced and at least partly formed by one's social, cultural and historical context, in ways that can only be partially transparent to the believer. Socialization is certainly essential to adopting and appropriating Christian belief and becoming accustomed to its practice and life. Although there are indeed people who acquire or maintain Christian beliefs through critical reflection and probing of their plausibility and viability, this is probably not the most widespread form of transmission of Christian faith. Furthermore, to the extent that Christian beliefs and practices are in fact also a result of reflection and reasoning and involve rational intention, this intentional rationality could refer to a much wider set of purposes and goals than formulating a belief in congruence with the sources of Christian faith. As Max Weber effectively taught us, approval of Christian beliefs might be related to a much wider set of purposes, for example possibilities for social mobility, for finding social bonds and connection, attaining social position or verifying one's belonging to the redeemed, than simply to be faithful to a particular religious tradition. Even though we acknowledge that Christian beliefs can not be reduced to effects of social context and structure, but also involve agents' rational intention, that intention can be considerably wider than formulating the content of Christian sources in a new situation and context.

But although beliefs clearly have these dimensions, it would hardly capture their nature to leave entirely out any dimension of reflection on their content and meaning in relation to a particular situation and context. Beliefs also involve interpretation through which something comes to attain a particular meaning and significance as related to a larger interpretive framework, or as integrated in a more comprehensive purpose and goal. That is not to say that human individuals have a natural propensity towards consistent and coherent systems of belief and understanding. Many of our beliefs are incoherent, fragmented bits and pieces that we live comfortably with, and which will not fit easily into an overarching, comprehensive system of beliefs. The view that we pursue consistency above all in the beliefs we hold, is unconvincing. Nonetheless, the possibility of a more limited view of how we interpret through the beliefs we hold, seems inescapable in order to explain why we hold the beliefs we do. That beliefs include at least some degree of reflection, for example of what certain central elements in Christian faith, such as belief in Christ, reconciliation, resurrection or neighborly love mean to someone in particular situations, seems to be a fairly sound assumption. People not only believe in God, they might have some idea about what or who this God is, the qualities of this God, and how it is possible to reconcile the existence of a God with other experiences of reality and human life. Clearly beliefs will involve reflections to a different degree for different people. Some people are more prone to reflect on and examine their beliefs and convictions than others, and some beliefs are more likely to stimulate such inspection. Still, the remaining point is that beliefs – at least some beliefs of some people – are not mere given facts, or a tacit backdrop of inarticulate assumptions. They also involve some kind of reflective activity and practice. In other words, they are not merely raw-material of critical, theological reflection. They also participate in that reflective activity.

It would miss the point and serve no purpose to level out the difference between theology as an academic, specialized and trained activity with inherent standards of conceptual clarity, methodological care and theoretical insight, and the kind of reflection implied by ordinary beliefs. Nonetheless, it seems more adequate to describe this as a difference in degree along a continuum of theological activity, rather than a difference in nature or kind. Claims to this effect have been offered by respectively Kathryn Tanner and Jeff Astley. Tanner's view of everyday theology and its constructive role in relation to the more specialized activity, starts in her view of culture as the dimension of social action that makes it socially meaningful, by virtue of the values, beliefs and symbols that permeate such actions. Theology, she claims, is the dimension that makes Christian practices and social action meaningful (Tanner, 1997: 70). It can be implicit, but also explicitly expressed in beliefs, exhortations, prayers, liturgies, preaching, etc. Ordinary life within Christian social practices occasions reflective investigation of beliefs, symbols and values, for example when situations or circumstances are difficult to reconcile with basic Christian commitments. This leads Tanner to conclude that "Despite these differences, an approach to theology as a part of Christian culture suggests that specialized theological investigation should be placed on a continuum with theological activity elsewhere, as something that arises in an "organic" way out of Christian practice" (Tanner, 1997: 71).

Astley, as mentioned above, applies the notion of "ordinary theology" to denote the "content, pattern and processes of ordinary people's articulation of the religious understanding", where "ordinary people" simply refers to those who have not received any particular theological training or education (Astley, 2002: 56). The point resembles Tanner's, namely how beliefs and values held by people within Christian religion's context are not mere, posited beliefs. They also involve the act of believing and therefore some measure of reflection, thinking and criticism. He joins Tanner in stating that the difference between ordinary theology, and the specialized, academically trained theology, is a difference of degree and not a difference of kind. But instead of Tanner's notion of a continuous spectrum, he describes their relation as dynamic.

This entails a view of beliefs as the object of empirical research rejected by Max Weber in his argument why empirical research ought not to be involved in normative propositions. Once, he says, allegedly normatively valid claims – such as religious beliefs, for example – becomes the object of empirical research, they lose their character as normative claims and are considered merely as existing facts, as stated rather than as potentially valid or true (Weber, 1999: 138–139). He rejects the possibility of studying them empirically as normative propositions. But thereby he leaves aside an important aspect of the object, namely the intention and purpose that partly defines it. This duality of perspectives has been famously described by Norwegian philosopher Hans Skjervheim, arguing that statements can be studied as facts and propositions. Studying them as propositions implies studying them as claims of validity, which may or may not be redeemed upon closer inspection and argumentation, whereas studying them as facts simply implies studying them as "brute data" (Taylor, 1985: 19), without any considerations to the claims they make (Skjervheim, 1996: 74). Studying beliefs as propositions rather than as brute data implies studying them under consideration of the normative claims they are making, and thereby to study them in terms of potentially invoking reasons and reflections attempting to back up that normative claim.

What makes actually held beliefs significant to normative reflection, is not the mere fact that they are held, but the reasons, intentions and interpretation involved in their being held. It is, so to speak, the everyday theological activity associated with them, which makes them potentially relevant to the normative reflection on the validity of beliefs. It is by virtue of being reflective of an activity that might relevantly resemble that of a more specialized theological reflection, that they are normatively significant. Some might object that resemblance alone is not sufficient. Hobby-ornithologists might make observations that resemble that of trained scientists, and yet it is rarely assumed that these observations add anything of particular value to biological science. Although the hobby-observations resemble the scientific ones, they are unlikely to offer anything that the methodologically and theoretically more advanced and sophisticated scientific practice could not provide itself, and with higher scientific merit. But the difference is that as ordinary beliefs involve interpretations, the data are partly constituted by the believer. The interpretation, reflection and reasons cannot be extracted from the belief itself, the way observation of avian behavior can be objectified and extracted from the observer.

Ordinary beliefs and normative theological reflection: Implying social constructivism?

The question that emerges from this view of ordinary beliefs as significant to normative reflection in theology concerns its epistemological assumptions, more specifically the relation between the underlying conception of justification of theological propositions, and the understanding of their nature and status. Does ascribing normative significance to ordinary beliefs and empirical research thereof wed theology to a non-realist view of the nature and status of theological propositions? For some, that would seem a small or no price, for others, a reason to discard the whole idea of considering ordinary beliefs as normatively significant for theological propositions. Without going into the discussion between realism and social constructivism, it is worthwhile to consider whether normative significance for empirical research of ordinary beliefs is incompatible with realist views of the nature of theological propositions. In the following I will use a parallel discussion in ethics to argue that it is not.

According to David Brink, two theories of justification have historically been the most influential: foundationalism and coherentism (Brink, 1989: 101). Foundationalism asserts that beliefs, such as for example moral or religious beliefs, can be justified – meaning that individuals seeking knowledge are warranted in sharing them – in one of two ways. A belief is justified either if it a) is a foundational belief, that is, self-justifying or non-inferentially justified, or if it is b) justified by an appropriate kind of inference from foundational beliefs. Even though these basic principles of justification allows for several variations, the essential characteristic of foundationalism is the idea that there are certain important beliefs, namely foundational beliefs, that are self-justifying and need no further justification or inference from a more fundamental principle.

Coherentism denies that any beliefs are self-justifying. According to coherentism a belief is justified insofar as it is part of a coherent system of beliefs, where the belief's coherence at least partially explains one's holding it (Brink, 1989: 103). Coherence is not simply a matter of logical consistency. It depends on a wider sense of comprehensiveness, where logical, but also probabilistic and explanatory relations between members of the coherent system are significant. This approach does not provide for a mechanical decision procedure according to which a belief's coherence can be determined, and consequently it is difficult to account for the exact and distinct properties that identify coherent beliefs. In spite of this indistinctness, the idea that beliefs have smaller or greater explanatory coherence and convincing force compared with other beliefs, seems fundamental to the way we go about in holding, questioning and accepting or discarding bodies of belief. Religious beliefs should not only be part of a system of religious beliefs, but of a system that comprises religious and non-religious beliefs alike. It seems fairly obvious that introducing ordinary beliefs into the justificatory process of normative propositions in theology, presupposes a coherentist theory of justification of beliefs rather than a foundationalist.

But this leads to the question whether theological propositions can then not be propositions about a reality independent of human practices of belief and justification, merely propositions about justificatory practices and beliefs. In short, does it wed theology to social constructivism and preclude realism as an overarching theory about the nature and status of theological propositions? Approaching the question in more general epistemological terms first, Brink asserts that coherentism is in fact fully compatible with realism, and for two reasons (Brink, 1989: 125–126). Firstly, the objectivist assumption about justification – which is a fundamental argument for claiming that coherentism requires that we abandon realism and prefer constructivism – is wrong. It starts from the claim that justification in holding a belief is justification in holding that belief to be true. But thereby objectivism exaggerates the connection between justification and truth. It ignores the distinction between knowledge, which implies truth, and justification, which does not. It is possible to be justified in a holding a false belief, and it makes sense to ask whether the belief I am justified in holding, is in fact true. Beliefs can be right or wrong for other reasons than their being justified according to a coherentist procedure of justification.

The second argument against the claim that coherentism requires us to abandon realism, suggests that justification might provide evidence of truth, by virtue of the role played by second-order beliefs. By holding beliefs, Brink asserts, we not only hold certain first-order beliefs about the world, human life and action, future, etc. We implicitly also hold certain second-order beliefs about our first-order beliefs, typically about the relationship between first-order beliefs and the external world that is their object. Second-order beliefs are beliefs about psychological makeup, cognitive and perceptual faculties, and the ways in which they attach to the external world. Combined with more comprehensive scientific theories, they form still other beliefs about reliability of mechanisms of forming beliefs. This way we come for example to hold the belief that certain beliefs deriving from observation, or from certain memories, are reliable, whereas beliefs about the future gained from palm reading are less reliable. Because these beliefs are beliefs about our relation to the external world that are metaphysically and conceptually independent of our evidence about it, second-order beliefs are also realist beliefs. A belief's coherence with a system of beliefs including also this kind of second-order beliefs, is evidence of the belief's truth. This way coherentism does not preclude realism, nor does it compel us to accept social constructivism as the broader theory of theological propositions (Brink, 1989: 127–130).

This could be further developed with regard to our main question by recalling how beliefs were considered to involve some measure of interpretation, meaning and intention. In short, beliefs also represent hermeneutic activity. This presents the question from a different angle, namely whether beliefs are thereby expressions of an inner self, and whether that is incompatible with them having some kind of hold in a reality external to human mind and consciousness. Hermeneutic thinking can, as William Schweiker asserts, be viewed as an heir to reflexive thinking (Schweiker, 1998: 76). It implicitly focuses on the individual's self-relation and self-reflection, exploring understanding and becoming aware of one's self. Interpretation and articulation occur through various media: typically language, but also gestures, arts and cultural forms. Seeing human understanding as a reflexive enterprise, enclosed in the shaping of meaning through media of understanding such as language or other kinds of symbolic systems, actualizes the question whether the human self is able to transcend its own limits in the act of understanding. Put differently, does it imply that all that human beings are really aware of, is human being, as what we take to be understanding of a reality is an exploration of our own attempts at symbolically orienting ourselves in reality? If this question is answered affirmatively, it implies that beliefs, values and imports ascribed through human meaning-making activity are effects of human linguistic freedom, that is: of human attempts at mastering reality by articulating understanding of it.

This is parallel to the problem discussed by Brink, whether propositions lend themselves to judgments of truth and falsity in virtue of evidence independently of the justifications offered in their favor. But the conclusion that beliefs about reality or value emerge solely from human, linguistic and articulating capacity and power is not a necessary one if we recognize how human interpretive activity is not simply a reflexive engagement in awareness of the inner self. It pursues awareness and understanding of the self in relation to what is not the self, what is other than the self. Already Schleiermacher – traditionally counted as the father of modern hermeneutics – accentuated in his analysis of structure of human life how no self-consciousness is possible without the presence of others, the "togetherbeing" with someone and something not ourselves. Reception rather than activity is fundamental to our existence as self-conscious subjects. The subject is constantly dependent upon something the possession of which is not under its own control (Schleiermacher, 1861: 9–20; cfr. also Schmidt, 1998: 91–97 for a more elaborate discussion of this point). The self in its freedom and activity is constituted by that which is not the self, that on which it depends. Our interpretations and articulations are also attempts at faithfully articulating import of something that are different from our reflexive capacities, in ways that are appropriate to the nature and reality of the situation or object in question. They lend themselves to the correction emerging from more accurate perceptions and grasps of import (Taylor, 1985: 75). We not only seek meaning of ourselves, but also of ourselves in relations to a reality outside ourselves (Schweiker, 1998: 69). Viewing religious beliefs as expressions of human interpretation and hermeneutical engagement with the world, and on that ground considering them significant to theological reflection and examination of normative propositions, does therefore not compel rejection of forms of realism – such as critical realism – as the broader theory of the status of theological propositions.

In sum, considering ordinary beliefs as significant for normative reflections on theology does not in itself compel us to abandon realist views of the status and nature of theological propositions in favor of social constructivist positions where justification for a proposition in a social context and through a social practice is evidence for the truth of that proposition.

Empirical research, beliefs and experiential adequacy as criteria for normative validity in theology

Realist conceptions of theological propositions are not only compatible with viewing ordinary beliefs as relevant to normative reflection. Critical realism, exemplifying realism within theology, might in fact explicate and justify this relevance of ordinary beliefs further. As a general epistemological theory critical realism claims that scientific theories and concepts relate and refer to a reality independent of human being and its perceptive and discursive practices, but that knowledge of this reality is shaped by linguistic conceptualization, including metaphors (Andersen et al., 2002: 230). This epistemological theory has been reformulated in relation to theology by among others J. Wentzel van Huyssteen, who suggests experiential adequacy as the most important epistemic value theologically rational propositions and beliefs must satisfy. On one hand this approach purports to take notice of the provisionality and social contextuality of theological propositions, but on the other seeks to respect their referential nature and attempts at making reliable cognitive claims (1997: 41). The point is to make human experiences, including religious experiences, the starting point for reflection on theological propositions as a basic epistemic warrant. Experiences, however, do not refer to an immediate access to a reality external to and independent of human life and practice, but is always interpreted experience, symbolically mediated through language, metaphors, but possibly also other forms of symbolic action such as gestures, art, etc. As such, critical realism is an empirical thesis. Theological reflection, v. Huyssteen suggests, begins with ordinary human experience and reflection, moving to religious affirmation about reality's nature (1997: 45). Theological propositions should be able to account for and accommodate such experiences, as attempts at grasping and encountering a reality external to human life, acknowledging that such propositions will always be provisional and principally open to further revision. Critical realism thus suggests that theology warrants its propositions on experiential grounds, that is, on attempts at interpreting and articulating experiences through language, metaphors and models. This does not contradict the role played by Scripture, and other essential Christian texts and expressions of theological history, but quite on the contrary recognizes their essential place and function in the interpretation and mediation of experiences.

This raises the question about whose experiences would be significant in warranting theological propositions, and how they can be accessed and assembled in order to ensure experiential adequacy. Ordinary beliefs could be viewed as already involving a certain evaluation of experiential adequacy, in the sense that people would be more likely to form, support and maintain beliefs they considered to be adequate to their experiences, and to discard or reject beliefs they perceived as experientially inadequate. In that perspective, ordinary beliefs are at least partly accompanied by or based on a consideration of their experiential adequacy. A more systematic inclusion of ordinary beliefs would thereby indirectly expand and solidify the experiential grounds from which theological propositions could be warranted. Rather than leaning mainly on the experiences of specialized theologians, or their assumptions about widespread, common experiences, it would expand theological propositions' epistemic basis in experiences. In this vein it would seem appropriate to allow considerations of actually held, ordinary beliefs – studied through empirical research – into the justificatory basis of theological propositions.

This resembles a point made by Astley, who asserts that including ordinary theology in critical, normative reflection of specialized theology in academia or church will corroborate its empirical fit (Astley, 2002: 149). It strengthens theology's grounding in experience, grounding it in a wider array of human experience tapped by including ordinary beliefs and the reflections and interpretation they involve. In this sense including ordinary beliefs in theological reflection is a possibility of increasing the experiential adequacy of its propositions.

To the extent that experiential adequacy is considered an important criterion for warranting normative propositions in theology, inclusion of ordinary beliefs might expand and strengthen their experiential adequacy by including a broader range of experience in normative propositions' epistemic warrant.

Normativity, criticism and empirical research of ordinary beliefs

A concern frequently raised in connection with ascribing normative significance to ordinary beliefs by including empirical research in specialized, theological reflection, is that it will prevent or obstruct criticism and innovation of those beliefs. By making them part of the basis which valid, normative propositions within theology has to meet, theological normativity becomes unable to criticize and innovate those existing beliefs in which it has immersed itself, the argument would suggest. Given that part of the task of theology is to reflect critically on the alleged validity of normative claims and so to defamiliarize us with the claims we have come to take for granted, ascribing normative significance to existing and already held beliefs will alienate theology from that task. Theology will fail its critical and innovative task by thus giving epistemological privilege to existing, ordinary beliefs.

This objection seems to rest on the premise that by including existing beliefs in the basis for theological normativity, one thereby also privileges the existing religious tradition over innovation and criticism. But this rests on the presupposition that ordinary beliefs either are prone to simply reiterate inherited and received beliefs without reflection or deliberation, or that, to the extent that they do reflect and reason about beliefs, they are less critical and innovative, and more affirmative of a dominant tradition of beliefs. The first objection implies that the line between reasoning and reflection on religious beliefs follows the line between ordinary beliefs and specialized theological reflection and reasoning. I have already argued that I believe that this is a mistaken assumption, although the degrees to and ways in which ordinary beliefs involve reflection are obviously very varied. The second implication of this objection seems to be that to the extent ordinary beliefs and reflections include reflections and reasoning, they will tilt towards the conventional, and privilege dominant, existing and received tradition. Change, criticism and revision must therefore be introduced by specialized and trained academic or ecclesial theology. This indirectly presupposes a specific conception of religious change. The presupposition is that critique, change and revision of religious tradition emerge as a result of specialized academic or ecclesial theological reflection, and not as the result of changes and criticisms in ordinary beliefs and their reflections. This is a rather one-sided and monolithic account of change to Christian traditions, which apparently implies that changes occur as a result of theological expertise's reflection and sanctioning. Criticisms and revisions of a religious tradition, according to this model, are stimulated and driven primarily by the specialized and trained reflections of academic or ecclesial theology. That, however, is a less plausible account of religious change. There is ample evidence that changes and revisions of Christian tradition and life have occurred as the result of complex processes where changes in believers' practices and convictions were followed by theoretically and intellectually trained reflection. On other occasions changes might have followed a different dynamic, starting by questioning and challenges within academically trained theology, opening up new pathways for understanding, belief and practice in religious communities. This is not the place to map the details of the complex terrain of religious change and criticism of Christian tradition, but it seems neglectful of the significance of social context for religious change to assume from the outset that change and criticism will predominantly be the effect of academic theology rather than that of ordinary beliefs and the reflections associated with them.

Some forms of contextual, liberationist theologies testify to this. Their claim is that beliefs and interpretations of and reflections on Christian tradition are reflective of the social position of power and privilege, respectively oppression and marginalization from where they emerge. But there is an asymmetry to this, in the sense that those in power have a privileged position which allows them to normalize their beliefs and practices as the preferable and valid ones. The dominant and prevailing set of beliefs is constructed from a position of privilege, dominance and power. Given the internalization and standardizing effects of such dominant sets of beliefs, which Miguel de la Torre explicates in terms of Pierre Bourdieu's concept of habitus, the ordinary beliefs' and practices' dominant position tends to be reinforced by their imprisoning of people's minds. As perpetuating dynamics of oppression and deprivation these dominant beliefs might exemplify ordinary beliefs that necessitate criticisms and revisions. But for contextual, liberationist theologies those opportunities for criticism are not found by searching for a de-contextualized basis for normativity, independent of the historical contingencies of ordinary beliefs. They are instead found by searching for an alternative position, by adopting the perspective and exploring the beliefs and practice of those who are disenfranchised and oppressed. The basis for criticism is identified not by abandoning ordinary beliefs, but by looking at the margins and fringes of the beliefs and practices that counter and resist dominant structures (de la Torre, 2004: 33–35). The basis for criticism, then, does not consist in inventing or constructing a position detached from and unaffected by ordinary beliefs and practices. It lies in the ability of being able to transpose oneself from a position associated with dominance and power to a position related to experiences of marginalization and oppression, and to recast theological normativity from the standpoint of the beliefs and practices that characterize that position.

Concrete empirical research and its potential, normative significance

After having considered epistemological and ethical questions connected with the use of empirical research of ordinary beliefs in normative, theological reflection, this final section will highlight some of the methodological and practical challenges that might confront us.

The first question is obviously how to specify and concretize what have so far been relatively unspecific formulations like empirical research potentially being "relevant to", "significant for" or "informing" normative reflection. There seems to be three main alternatives. One position would require that valid normative propositions must conform to what empirical research shows us regarding ordinary beliefs. This requirement is unwarranted for a number of reasons. As will be exemplified below, empirically described beliefs are often too diverse and variegated to provide a uniform and unequivocal standard of measure of normative propositions. Secondly, it would confine the range of relevant reasons and the justificatory basis for critical and systematic assessment of normative propositions. It would exclude reasons produced through sources such as more systematic inclusion of insights into vital sources of a Christian tradition, or knowledge provided through other sciences, both of which would also require expertise and skill to analyze, understand and evaluate in relation to their normative significance. Valid normative propositions cannot simply be deduced from ordinary beliefs, as a systematic account and summary of beliefs that are held at a given time.

The other extreme would be to allow empirical research of ordinary beliefs to support and corroborate what is already known through theoretically based normative reflection, informed by sources independent of ordinary beliefs. This model would require that valid normative propositions conform to and be developed on the basis of theoretical reflection on basic theories and central doctrines and sources (Scripture, ecclesial tradition, science, rationality), but allow that they be colored or inspired by ordinary beliefs to the extent that they do not conflict with comprehensive theories. This position would in effect preclude the idea that empirical research of ordinary beliefs can have any independent normative significance, apart from the insights already provided through theoretical reflection or confined to the area left open by the silence of more comprehensive theories. In this sense this model seems to circumvent the whole issue by insisting that reflection based on sources other than actual, ordinary beliefs, take precedence in determining valid, normative claims. For this reason it is not really pertinent to the present discussion and issue at hand.

A third model would unsurprisingly be a middle way between the two already described, and require some sort of balance between insights provided by empirical research of ordinary beliefs, and insights made available through more comprehensive theories and sources. This model would advocate a state of balance between ordinary beliefs on one hand, and comprehensive theories developed from other sources, such as Scripture, ecclesial tradition and doctrines, and science, on the other. This would be the theological "equivalent" of the Rawlsian notion of reflective equilibrium, as a state of equilibrium between our considered judgments

– beliefs – in concrete cases, and broader theories concerning human life and morality. Tentatively this model would imply that normative propositions be validated through a process of critical reflection that moves back and forth between on one hand ordinary beliefs, and on the other essential theories or interpretive frames. The latter would partly consist of the grammar that structures and regulates expressions of faith within a given tradition. Within a Lutheran tradition such elements as law and gospel as the two ways God addresses human being and reality, justification by faith as defining human fulfillment, or human beings' innate capacity for moral cognition, would probably be essential. And partly it would contain established scientific paradigms and the basic insights they have generated about reality and human life. The process of critically reflecting on normative propositions in order to establish their validity, could then be described as a hermeneutical process, searching for the best fit between concrete, ordinary beliefs, and a wider interpretive framework, and where discrepancies would be solved by either suggesting that ordinary beliefs be adjusted, or that an element to the wider, comprehensive interpretive framework needs adjustment. The benefit of this model is that it ascribes significance to ordinary beliefs, described through empirical research, as well as to basic theoretical interpretive frameworks developed through Christian tradition as well as sciences, in the critical reflection on normative propositions. Rather than consistently privileging the one over the other, it recommends a hermeneutical process of discernment as the appropriate pathway to determining valid normative claims.

Is this model viable? Which questions would confront us by attempting to use it as an "instrument" to determine the normative implications of empirical research of ordinary beliefs? I will use as an example three different survey studies, each mapping beliefs in God in various groups.

The international social survey programme (ISSP) conducts annual surveys on various topics in national, representative samples in European countries, including Norway. Religion was the topic in the year 1991, 1998 and 2008. Some, but not all questions, were identical in these three surveys, providing an opportunity for analyzing change and tendencies. Among other things, these surveys asked respondents about their belief in God, their religious practices and participation, and their religious self-identification. It also asked questions about more alternative religious beliefs and practices, less associated with established and traditional religious communities and institutions. One of the tendencies shown by the data in this survey through the three years is a general decline in belief in God, but especially a decline in more absolutist formulated beliefs in God, such as "I know that God exists and have no doubts about it". In 1991 this statement was supported by 20 percent, one out of five, whereas it has sunk to 15 percent in 2008. On the other hand, explicit rejections of the existence of a God increase, from 10 percent in 1991, to 18 percent in 2008. These tendencies are manifest also among churchgoers, although to a less degree. Should this kind of data feed into critical reflection on normative propositions regarding God and God's nature and qualities? Could and should theological reflection on God and who God is, be informed by how people believe in God and how they articulate this belief?

This immediately points towards some methodological problems. The beliefs empirically described here are heterogeneous and diversified, which evokes the simple question which beliefs ought to be included in normative reflection on valid propositions regarding belief in God. Based on the "reflective balance"-model above, it seems likely to include those beliefs that will most easily yield a state of equilibrium with the comprehensive theories and grammar of faith, which would probably be the absolutist version of certain belief in God. But one could also make the claim that in order to explore more critical and innovative formulations of belief, the less conformist formulations ought to be inserted in the reflective equilibrium model.

Another way out of this problem would be to pose further conditions on the kind of actual, ordinary beliefs that could legitimately be included in normative reflection. At least three alternatives could be considered. One would be to claim the support of a clear majority in order to consider ordinary beliefs to be relevant to normative reflection. This seems to resemble Astley's model, which argues that it is the widespread support of beliefs in a context of believers that make these beliefs consequential to normative reflection. But this solution will prevent the inclusion of beliefs that develop at the margins among smaller groups, and thus hamper a critical and innovative perspective in favour of a conventionalist one. A second would be to claim that not just any ordinary beliefs ought to be accommodated by normative reflection, but only those that are well-considered, emerge from a minimum of knowledge of and familiarity with Christian tradition and doctrine. Considering the parallel to the Rawlsian notion, reflective equilibrium should persist between our *considered judgments* and the more comprehensive theories. Considered judgment would refer to their being the result of some degree of informed reflection, stripped of undue self-interests, delusions, misperceptions etc., not just any intuition that came into our head. The problem is to distinguish well-considered beliefs from the unconsidered ones, and where to set the threshold.

A third possibility would be to define more specifically the context or group whose beliefs would be relevant. The ISSP-surveys are carried out in national samples, irrespective of church-membership or -participation, and some might claim that only the beliefs of people who belong to and identify with a given context of faith would be relevant. This could be exemplified by another survey, carried out some years ago in a representative sample of members of Church of Norway (Høeg et al 2000).

This survey testifies to a considerable difference in support of beliefs, conditional on the respondents' degree of participation and sense of belonging to Church of Norway. Of those who attend church services at least once a month (often used as an indicator of frequent church attendance in Norway) 63 percent believe that God really exists and they have no doubt about it (N=158). Among those who attend church several times a year, 31 percent believes without doubt that God really exists (N=407). And 27 percent of those attending church at least once a month sense that although in doubt they feel they believe in God, whereas this is the case for 35 percent of those who attend church services several times during the year. The similar group of church-goers was asked which proposition regarding Jesus Christ fit to their beliefs. 78 percent of the frequent church goers (attending at least once a month) said that the statement "Jesus is my savior, who died for my sins" fit well with their beliefs (N= 158), whereas 39 percent of the more rare church-goers (several times a year) believed this statements fit their belief (N=407). The statement "Jesus showed us that God loves us" was recognized by 66 percent of the frequent church-goers to fit their beliefs, and by 61 percent of the more occasional church-goers to correspond to their beliefs about Jesus. In sum, the frequent church-goers identified to a larger degree than the more occasional church-attendants with the traditionalist description of Jesus. These differences were much less clear regarding the descriptions that described Jesus in more "friendly" and human terms as the one who showed us that God loves us, and permitted doubt as an integral part of belief in God.

A similar pattern is revealed if instead of church-going we use sense of belonging to the Church of Norway as the independent variable. Among those with a very strong sense of belonging to Church of Norway, 66 percent (N=104) believe without doubt that God really exists, whereas among those with a relatively strong sense of belonging to the Church of Norway, 32 percent believe without doubt that God exists (N=618). When it comes to a more doubting belief in God the picture is reversed. 19 percent of those with a very strong sense of belonging feel that although they doubt, they do believe in God, whereas 40 percent of those with a relatively strong sense of belonging feel they believe in God even though they doubt. And among those with a very strong sense of belonging to the Church of Norway, 79 percent support the statement "Jesus is my savior who dies for my sins", whereas this is the case for 43 percent of those with a relatively strong sense of belonging.

The difference between these two groups diminishes when we look instead on the statement "Jesus showed us that God loves us", supported by 68 percent of those with a very strong sense of belonging, and 51 percent of those with a relatively strong sense of belonging. This demonstrates perceptible differences in beliefs between groups who are connected with the church; however all has a minimum degree of connection. The stronger and tighter the connection with the church, the larger is the familiarity and identification with the more traditionalist and the absolutist expressions of beliefs.

This point can be further emphasized by invoking a survey study among elected members of local parish councils in Church of Norway (Schmidt 2011). These are conventionally considered to form a group of church members with a tight relation to the church, constituting a "core group" of members. A survey conducted in 2010 in order to analyze their background as well as their experiences and evaluations of having this voluntary task largely confirms this image. Among council-members, 59 percent believe without doubt that God really exists, and 29 percent feel they believe in God, although they have doubts. 78 percent stated that the statement "Jesus is my savior who died for my sins" fit their beliefs, and 83 percent identified with the statement "Jesus showed that God loves us".

These last two surveys, among church-members and among elected members of local parish councils, demonstrate how beliefs vary dependent on one's degree of identification with and participation in the church. Would it be adequate to include the beliefs of those who identify the strongest with the church, into the reflective process towards a reflective equilibrium where normative claims would be justified as warranted? This strategy would yield a similar problem to the one mentioned above, namely that critical and innovative potential of ordinary beliefs would be more likely to go unnoticed. Recall the point that this potential would be more likely to become articulate at the margins and fringes of a given community of interpretation.

It seems to be hard to find a methodologically plausible and transparent way to incorporate empirically researched actual, ordinary beliefs into normative reflection, in a way that preserves a critical and innovative potential on one hand, and on the other avoids arbitrariness in the inferred implications.

Conclusion

The denial of including empirical research of people's beliefs, conduct and commitments into normative reflection has traditionally been fuelled by the understanding that this would be epistemologically as well as ethically unsound. It would imply abandoning any external reference for theological normative propositions, and it would obstruct the basis for criticism of prejudiced and biased normative assumptions. However, whereas neither epistemological nor ethical reasons represent insurmountable objections against considering empirical research of beliefs as relevant to normative reflection in Christian theology, the methodological difficulties in doing so in a transparent and systematic way are considerable.

References

Andersen, Svend; Grønkjær, Niels and Nørager Troels, *Religionsfilosofi. Kristendom og tænkning* [Philosophy of religion. Christianity and thought]. København: Gads Forlag, 2002.
Astley, Jeff, *Ordinary Theology. Looking, Listening and Learning in Theology*. Aldershot: Ashgate Publ., 2002.
Brink, David, *Moral Realism and the Foundations of Ethics*. Cambridge: Cambridge U.P., 1989.
De La Torre, Miguel A. *Doing Christian Ethics from the Margins,*. Maryknoll: Orbis Books, 2004.
Dreyer, Jaco S. "Theological Normativity: Ideology or Utopia? Reflections on the Possible Contribution of Empirical Research", In: Van der Ven, Johannes and Michael Scherer-Rath (eds.), *Normativity and Empirical Research in Theology*. Leiden: Brill 2005.
Ganzevoort, R. Ruard, "What you see is what you get. Social construction and normativity in practical theology". In: Van der Ven, Johannes and Michael Scherer-Rath (Eds.), *Normativity and Empirical Research in Theology*. Leiden: Brill. 17–34, 2005.

Henriksen, Jan-Olav, "Researching theological normativity. Some critical and constructive suggestions." *Studia Theologica. Nordic Journal of Theology.* Vol 60. 207–220, 2006.

Høeg, Ida Marie, Harald Hegstad, Ole Gunnar Winsnes, *Folkekirke 2000 [People's church 2000]*. Oslo: Stiftelsen Kirkeforskning, 2000.

Korsgaard, Christine, *The Sources of Normativity*. Cambridge: Cambridge U.P., 1996.

Lewis, Thomas A., "Ethnography, anthropology, and comparative religious ethics: Or ethnography and the comparative ethics local." *Journal of Religious Ethics*. Vol 38 (3). 395–403, 2010.

Schleiermacher, Friedrich Daniel Ernst, *Der Christliche Glaube nach den Grundsätzen der evangelischen Kirche im Zusammenhange dargestellt*. Bd I (2. Ausg., 1830). Berlin: Georg Reimer, 1861.

Schmidt, Ulla, *Normativity and Reality. A Study of the Ethical Demand in Human Life-Reality, with special regard to the ethical theory of Trutz Rendtorff*. Oslo: Doctoral thesis, 1998.

Schmidt, Ulla, "Christian ethics and empirical research." *Studia Theologica. Nordic Journal of Theology*. Vol 63 (2009). 67–88.

Schmidt, Ulla, *Menighetsrådsmedlemmer og menighetsråd i Den norske kirke [Council members and parish councils in Church of Norway]*. KIFOnotat 1/2011. Oslo: Stiftelsen Kirkeforskning.

Schweiker, William, *Power, Value, and Conviction. Theological Ethics in the Postmodern Age*. Cleveland: The Pilgrim Press, 1998.

Schweitzer, Friedrich, "Which normativity and what kind of empirical research? From dualism to multiple interplays". In: Van der Ven, Johannes and Michael Scherer-Rath (Eds.), *Normativity and Empirical Research in Theology*. Leiden: Brill. 85–100, 2005.

Skjervheim, Hans, *Deltakar og tilskodar og andre essays [Participant and observer and other essays]*. Oslo: Aschehoug, 1996.

Tanner, Kathryn, *Theories of Culture. A New Agenda for Theology*. Minneapolis: Fortress Press, 1997.

Taylor, Charles, *Philosophy and the Human Sciences. Philosophical Papers 2*. Cambridge: Cambridge U.P., 1985

Van der Ven, Johannes, "An Empirical or a Normative Approach to Practical-theological Research. A False Dilemma". In: Van der Ven, Johannes and Michael Scherer-Rath (Eds.), *Normativity and Empirical Research in Theology*. Leiden: Brill. 101–136, 2005.

Van Huyssteen, J. Wentzel, "Critical Realism and God: Can there be Faith after Foundationalism?" In: van Huyssteen, J. Wentzel, *Essays in Postfoundationalist Theology*. Grand Rapids: Wm. B. Eerdmans, 1997, 40–52.

Weber, Max, *Verdi og handling [Value and action]*. (Sel. and transl. from *Gesammelte Aufsätze zur Wissenschaftslehre*). Oslo: Pax Forlag 1999.

Normative evaluations in theological ethics

Paul Leer-Salvesen

Normativity, freedom and loyalty

Most scholars agree that philosophy and theology are normative sciences. We may have different opinions about how to establish normative evaluations and what sort of authorities we use to come to normative conclusions. But it is not too much to say that there is a consensus in the academic world that philosophy and theology are normative disciplines. Philosophers and theologians describe and analyze, but their task is not limited to description: They have something to say about what is true and false, at least about validity and plausibility. They consider what is good and evil, right and wrong. They draw normative conclusions.

In different periods of time scholars have discussed whether philosophy and theology are real sciences when they insist on their normative tasks. My impression is that this discussion is not very much alive today. The borderline between normative and descriptive sciences is not so clear as scholars proclaimed when positivism was booming. Most social scientists, for example, will admit that there is room for normative evaluations in their work, and theologians and moral philosophers use descriptive tools and empirical methods in their work. There are and should be differences, but it is far too easy to say that social sciences are descriptive and philosophy and theology normative. It is more interesting to discuss which categories of normativity we accept in academic scholarship.

I will make the following assertion: Academic work is always critical. Normativity which excludes criticism is no longer academic. Philosophers and theologians draw conclusions about what is true or false, good or evil, but they should be able to do so with a high degree of freedom. Conclusions drawn in blind obedience to authorities outside the academic discourse are problematic. When normative evaluations occur in the academic field, and moreover in politics and in pluralistic democracies, they have to be tested in open and critical discourses. We can use the famous phrase from Jürgen Habermas to illustrate this point: "The power of the better arguments" shall influence which normative evaluation can be plausible, and which not.[1]

The phenomenon of normativity has in some traditions, and especially in some religious milieus, been understood as a force which demands obedience: You shall obey the doctrine written by the authority. This is a position which opposes central values in science and academic work, such as freedom of thought and speech, and also the obligation to stand up and speak and write in accordance with your conviction.

In ethics it is important to recognize the difference between obedience and loyalty. Far too often these two virtues are mistaken for being one and the same. Obedience is blind, and it occurs most frequently in the upwards relation to the father, the leader, the undisputed authority. Loyalty is seeing, rooted in values, and critical. A moral subject will always have several loyalties at the same time: Upwards towards the leader, the owners, the board, but also in the relations to colleagues, peers, students, patients, clients, the civil society and not to forget: Your own life world with the values, standards and beliefs you are committed to in other fields of life than your work life. To place the normative evaluations only in one of these loyalties or relations is a dangerous option. Of course it hurts when different loyalties crash. Moral ambivalence is painful, but this pain may be a sign of good moral health. Zygmunt Baumann has made this point in several articles, reminding us about the complexity of the different challenges we meet as moral subjects. He says:

> At the moral party of two, I and the Other arrive derobed from our social trappings, stripped of status, social distinctions, handicaps, positions, or roles, neither rich nor poor, high or lowly, mighty or disempowered – reduced to the bare essentiality of our common humanity. The moral self is constituted inside such a space cannot but feel uncomfortable the moment the moral party of two is broken into by the Third. [2]

To sum up this point: Normative evaluations are necessary in science, and important characteristics of philosophy, ethics and theology. But in the academic field normativity is always combined with a free and critical dis-

---

1 Jürgen Habermas: "Eine genealogische Betrachtung zum kognitiven Gehalt der Moral" in: *Die Einbeziehung des Anderen*, Suhrkamp Verlag, Frankfurt am Main 1996.
2 Zygmunt Bauman: "Morality Begins at Home" in: Harald Jodalen and Arne Johan Vetlesen: *Closeness: An Ethics*. Scandinavian University Press, Oslo Oxford 1997 p. 218

course. A scholar can never be blind and obedient to an authority outside or above the discourse. She has to handle her different loyalties when it comes to normative evaluations, arguing for her stands, with an open mind for nuances and counterarguments. Even if it hurts! It may be painful when you meet contradicting challenges and claims from different loyalties or authorities. But this pain is a necessary one, emerging from the essence of being a moral subject in the world.

David Hume on *is* and *ought*

Social sciences, philosophy, ethics and theology are more closely related today than 50 years ago. Most scholars will agree that they share the challenge of including normativity in their work, and that the position of value neutrality is very difficult, perhaps even impossible also for a sociologist or social anthropologist. We can see that other differences between scholars in social sciences and humanities are broken up: They often refer to the same theories in their work, and they may use the same methods in research. You can no longer simply say that a theological and ethical work is done at the desk, sociologists and anthropologists leave the office to do fieldwork and interviews. Today many ethicists and theologians include empirical methods in their work. And this is challenging: How can we use empirical findings in theological and ethical discourses?

We have to pay attention to some classic sentences about normativity and description, written by David Hume in his famous book *A Treatise of Human Nature* in 1738[3]. These sentences have followed me since I was a young student in my first semester in philosophy, and I still don't know whether I fully understand them. David Hume warned against normative conclusions drawn from "is" to "ought", I learned as a student. And I still meet the same warning as a professor and supervisor of PhD projects in empirical ethics today: Hume says that you cannot jump from "is" to "ought" – how can you and your PhD students then use fieldwork, interviews and surveys in ethical research, and use the material to draw normative conclusions? Shouldn't the heritage from Hume be interpreted in a way that leaves normativity to philosophers and descriptions and empirical work to social scientists? Maybe I'm creating a caricature, but sometimes I hear these reflections used as critique of empirical research in eth-

---

3   David Hume: *A treatise of human nature*. Oxford University Press Oxford 2000.

ics and theology: Leave "ought" to the philosophers and "is" to the social scientists. Don't mix the two!

It is true that Hume warns against conclusions drawn from "is" to "ought". But the way I read him, this is not a general warning against normative moral conclusions, and it is certainly not a warning against use of experience and empirical material in moral discourses. Hume's agenda is another one. First of all he is skeptical towards every attempt to make universal statements about how nature is in itself and as such. His point is a warning against universalism, and against the hegemonic role of cognitivism in philosophy and ethics. For him it is impossible to say: I know how nature is, therefore I can tell what good life is. Knowledge about nature is preliminary for Hume, and is changing. It is impossible once and for all to state how nature is, and therefore it is not possible to draw universal and certain conclusions from natural institutions or laws to how we shall live our lives as human beings in the world.

I see that it is possible to understand Hume as a "noncognitivist", but I find it more interesting to read him in a different way: In ethics we cannot rely on reason alone. We have to build a moral theory which includes passions and virtues[4]. Therefore studies in ethics are different from studies in natural sciences. We need other instruments than reason alone. We need to get access to people's "life-world", to use a phrase from Habermas. And then we have to listen to them and study how they live their moral lives.

Allow me a modern example to illustrate the difficulty of bringing knowledge about nature into ethical discourse: Some participants in the ongoing debate about same-sex-marriage argue in the following way: We know from nature (or from the theology of orders of creation) that humans exists as male and female, longing for each other and sexual fulfillment in reproduction. This knowledge leads some theologians and ethicists to the conclusion that same-sex marriage is unnatural: Nature is heterosexual as such, is then the undisputed condition. Therefore ethics and laws both in society and churches have to ban and forbid same-sex-marriages. I see that this way of bringing Hume into the contemporary debate comes close to ordering a taxi to Forum Romanum, but the point is the following: Hume warns against use of knowledge about nature as normative arguments in ethical discourses because our knowledge about nature is always fragmentary and shifting.

---

4   *Treatise* Book 2.1.1.1.

"Morality consists not in any *matter of fact*, which can be discovered by the *understanding*," Hume writes[5]. Two terms are important here: By *matter of fact* he means phenomena we can observe and study with the intention to draw general conclusions about how things work. Hume is skeptical towards this epistemological position in general, but especially in ethics. Some philosophers say that for Hume, there are no moral facts at all, that he is a consequent relativist. But others conclude that there are moral facts in Hume's world, but not of the kind that can be observed by reason, as opposed, say, to direct perception. "Vice and virtue," Hume writes, "may be compared to sounds, colors, heat and cold, which according to modern philosophy, are not qualities in objects, but perceptions in the mind."[6]

The second important term is *understanding*. Hume opposes the strong position of *ratio* in moral philosophy, from Plato to modern philosophy. He argues for the important influence of *feelings and emotions* in ethics and morality, especially phenomena as *compassion* or *sympathy* and *empathy*. These important terms in moral philosophy Hume calls *fellow feeling*, which enables us to rejoice when others succeed, not only when we achieve advantages ourselves. At this point we can observe a similarity with much later philosophers, such as Emmanuel Levinas or Knut E. Løgstrup, who emphasize the priority of the virtue *unselfishness* and the importance of the concept of *otherness* in moral life and in ethics.

Ratio is for Hume an insufficient instrument for navigation in moral life. But reason is still important. We must, however, include studies of passions and virtues in ethics. "Reason alone can never be a motive to any action of the will",[7] he claims. Instead of the impossible task of building rational ethics on universal principles and observation of how nature is, Hume simply recommends that we study how good people have lived their good lives and what they have considered as good and evil. Through this sort of ethical studies, Hume opens up for empirical studies in ethics and theology, and makes room for including people's *experiences* in normative evaluations. Not in form of universal statements about how things *are* as *matters of fact*, but more particular: We have to study and tell narratives about how people have lived their lives and how they dealt with ethical problems and dilemmas. These narratives and ethical case studies

---

5 *Treatise* Book 3, p. 469.
6 Anthony Appiah Kwame: *Experiments in Ethics*. Harvard University Press, Cambridge 2008, p. 212.
7 *Treatise* Book 3, p. 413.

are relevant resources in contemporary ethical discourses. Isn't this a key point in what we can call *empirical informed ethics research*?

Allow me one example from Christian ethics: The letters of Paul are important sources in Christian ethics. In some traditions Christians argue in the following way: "Paul has said... Thus, we ought to ..." This is one example of universal conclusions drawn from "is" to "ought" which exclude experience, passions and virtues from the ethical discourse. A more fruitful way of using Paul in contemporary Christian ethics could be this: "Paul has said and done …. Let us listen to it and consider whether it still makes sense as true and good in our churches and lives today." In the latter approach, we do not simply relate to Paul as a formal moral authority, but as one who supplies us with grounds and reasons that we still have to consider and assess.

Normativity and authorities

We have claimed that normative evaluations defend their place in academia. Not only in sciences as philosophy and theology, but also in social sciences and in empirical research on ethics. We have also claimed that academic normativity is critical and open to better arguments. Normative academic stands are not fixed once and for all, and they are never to be dictated from an external authority. An academic cannot let the pope, the board, the guru or the ayatollah have the last world in disputed matters. He can of course listen to the religious leader and consider the stand and arguments coming from this authority. But a true scholar is always free to criticize the pope. Academic normativity is always combined with values of free thought and free speech, and virtues of open-mindedness and willingness to listen to others.

What then about normativity in churches and religious communities? Is normativity here of a completely different kind than in academic institutions? This is a big question, and a difficult one. First of all because the notion "religious communities" is quite a mouthful. It spans from a liberal modern Christian church in north-west Europe to Catholic institutions in Rome, or guru-led religious societies in India. The questions of normativity and authority will look very different in these contexts. To make it a bit easier for me, I will concentrate on my own Christian tradition.

The history of Christian ethics is both a history of how to live with different ethical stands and practices in pluralities with various degrees of tension, and a history of totalitarianism where patriarchs try to discipline and control the opposition, banning critics and heretics. Church history is a brave history of how people managed to live together in peace in spite of important and threatening differences, and a sad history of how authorities used power and violence to silence alternative thinkers. The situation for critical theologians and ethicists are of course a much better one in both church and society today: Plurality has arrived, both in academia and in the churches. But we are still facing some challenges:

In the years 2001 to 2003 we had a discussion about freedom in academic theological research in Norway. The background was Professor Jan-Olav Henriksen's texts about homosexual partnership. The problem discussed was whether a professor in a private theological school (The Norwegian School of Theology) has the right, and maybe also the obligation, to publish results from his own research, even if they differ from the official ethical stands of his faculty: Jan-Olav Henriksen defended homosexual partnership and argued that it is possible to give reason for this stand in Christian ethics. The board of his school disagreed. Could he still publish the results of his theological and ethical research and keep his job as a professor in the school?

There is good reason to say that this conflict showed how different loyalties can crash, and also how different normative conducts can come into conflict. The question was whether a theological researcher in a private theological school is obligated by other normative loyalties than academics and scholars in theological departments at the state universities.

Academic theologians from several Nordic countries took part in the discussion. In a hearing in The Academy of Sciences and Letters in Oslo,[8] Professor Svend Andersen from Aarhus made a comment on *"The normativity of theology".* He used some distinctions inspired by Jürgen Habermas[9] to distinguish between three different sorts of normativity in academic scholarship and theological ethics:

The first Andersen calls "professional normativity" (faglig normativitet in Danish). In every guild of researchers, we find both written and unwritten rules and standards of professional ethics and research ethics. Some of the rules have become juridical, and they are included in national and

---

8   Texts from this hearing are published by "Den nasjonale forskningsetiske komite for samfunnsvitenskap og humaniora": *Akademisk frihet i teologisk forskning* Oslo 2003, Vol 3.
9   Jürgen Habermas: *Theorie des kommunikativen Handelns,* Suhrkamp, Frankfurt am Main 1981.

international laws. Others are guidelines and standards of conduct, formulated and practiced by the academic world and scholarship itself. Just one parenthesis here: There is now a tendency towards more laws and jurisprudence in research ethics, and less free ethical discourses. The conducts of research ethics is to an increasing degree being converted to law in the Nordic countries and in the EU. But that is a different topic. The question about how much of moral life we decide to regulate by law and threats of punishment, and how much we want to keep in free and open ethical discourses, where we seldom punish, normally only formulate disapprovals, is an important issue. The point in this context is the following: Every scholar and researcher, and of course every theological and philosophical ethicist, has to recognize some normative standards for good and bad research. He is not free to do whatever he wants. The end neither hallows nor sanctifies the means in academic research, and some values are undisputed. As the case about the British historian David Irving shows us: There are some normative standards in the guild of historians which say that a scholar can't deny the Holocaust. Other sciences have similar unwritten rules – expressions of a consensus in the guild or the profession. This is explicit normativity and the guild claims loyalty from the members. It can be called "academic" or "professional" normativity.

The second normativity Svend Andersen identifies, he calls "authority grounded normativity" ("autoritetsbegrunnet normativitet" in Danish). This is a complicated topic. We could mention the whole history of how universities liberated themselves from control and censorship from religious authorities, under this point. We can also tell contemporary stories about the influence of institutions in the Vatican over academic Catholic theology worldwide, not only in the church led seminars for education of priests. It is not only the Norwegian School of Theology which has a history of using externally grounded authority to formulate normativity and try to discipline its scholars. The conflict in this Norwegian institution is solved now, but this is still a hot topic in many theological institutions world-wide, and it is a matter of great concern for individual theological scholars: How can some of us for example combine the role as free theological researchers with the role as ordained priests? Could the bishop look into my research, as a bishop? Do the promises I gave at the ordination have any impact on what I can express or publish as a scholar?

Svend Andersen is crystal clear: Theological research cannot be governed by a normativity grounded in an external and formal authority. The pope, the owners of a school or the bishops cannot use any sort of force to influence the work in academic theology. Of course they can take part in the discussion and dispute whether a certain conclusion in theology or ethics is inside or outside the doctrine of the church. It is the job of the church leaders to do that! But they cannot use censorship or index and try to remove the theological scholar from his position. Academic scholarship is per definition free. If theology is submitted to an authority grounded normativity which makes it possible to fire a theological scholar because he concludes differently from the church in a disputed ethical matter, it is no longer free academic theology. I agree with Svend Andersen, but later I will show that it is not only theology which experiences these challenges from external authorities. This question is a complicated one for several scholars who have a close relationship to conflicts and tensions in culture and society.

The third form of normativity Andersen identifies, he calls "the normativity of plausibility" ("gyldighetsnormativitet" in Danish), and here we recognize the voice of Jürgen Habermas and his "Theorie des Kommunikativen Handelns". The point is that a science which examines a topic without any interest in the questions of truth and plausibility, is a descriptive science. Maybe some scholars will still say that Science of Religion comes close to this kind of science, trying not to make normative evaluations about right and wrong, true and false within a religion. But the position is hard to keep, even for a scholar who brings with him the heritage from positivism. Theology and Philosophy, however, are interested in the questions of truth and good and right. Their scholars make normative evaluations. But Svend Andersen is of the opinion that an academic theologian shall not say or preach what is true or false. *The preaching she should leave to the church itself. She shall evaluate what could be possible pretentions of plausibility and truth – and what is not plausible.* The last steps into the normative preaching she should leave to the priests and the other members of the church who are responsible for the church doctrine: She can recommend what are possible theological or ethical positions in the church, but not make the choice on behalf of the church. One further reason for this is that academic theology shall always be critical, pluralistic and moving. Once again: Normative evaluations of plausibility are still an important task for academic theologians, but they shall not act as if they were bishops.

Here, there is an interesting parallel to studies of law and jurisprudence. The scholars studying law at the university can come up with research based conclusions on how to interpret the law in a particular situation, and of course also on how we cannot interpret a certain paragraph. But the scholar has to leave the specific judgment to the judges in court.

The scholars analyze and criticize and watch over the jurisprudence, but they are not responsible for what is going on in the courtrooms. There are some fascinating similarities between scholars in theology and law on one side, and practicing judges and priests on the other. The first group shall interpret, analyze and come up with suggestions which may also contain normative evaluations. The second group shall judge and preach and stands much closer to the situation were practice is influenced and changed.

In the world of Habermas, plurality is a word of honor, not a threat. It is by help of free and open theological or ethical and philosophical dialogues that we can come closer to say something about good and evil, true and false, right and wrong. Following Habermas, theological ethics and other normative sciences cannot be bound and gagged by external authorities that dictate what is true or false, right and wrong. Academic scholarship shall always be critical and free to express its thoughts and suggestions and conclusions. Academic scholarship is also recognized by plurality and the coexistence of different views and thoughts which meet in free and open discussions where the power of the better arguments rules.

I mentioned that the challenge of external authorities is not only a theological issue. We find similar challenges in other disciplines, especially in sciences which include different degrees of social commitment in their scholarship. Criminology and victimology are scholarly disciplines which arose in milieus characterized by solidarity and commitment to oppressed groups. Gender studies as well. Criminologists and gender researchers often perform their research in close contact with milieus outside academia. The scholars may share the worldview and values of the "believers" outside, and they tend to listen to them and be influenced by them. Maybe there is a parallel in some kinds of contextual theology, influenced by liberation theology. Several scientists are under influence of authorities in society, or at least values and norms in milieus outside the universities.

I cannot see anything wrong in this, as long as academic work continues to be critical. But scholars who define themselves as obedient servants of external authorities are no longer performing free academic scholarship. Scholars are not preachers. Scholars are not judges. But still they can make suggestions about different types of plausible norms and deliver critical remarks and conclusions based on analyzes. They can be normative!

Empirically informed ethics

I began with David Hume and his warning against ethics constructed from universal principles. Hume is nevertheless normative. He still makes normative evaluations in his ethics. But his way into normativity is different from the analytic and rationalistic traditions. Hume recommends that we study "how good people live their good lives", and that we listen to what he with a wonderful word calls *the fellow feeling*. Therefore I think he is an interesting philosopher for researchers who try to combine empirical work with philosophical and theological analyzes. With his strong emphasis on experience as valuable in ethics he also opens up for a dialectical relationship between academia and society.

Of course we shall also be critical against our empirical findings. Every proclamation of normativity has to be examined carefully, whether it comes from the desk of a scholar or from a church or an activist group. Normative voices have to be met with critical, ethical reflection. The ideal situation is that this reflection happens in a pluralistic group and ethical discourse as Jürgen Habermas suggests. Habermas recommends that those who participate in the dialogue shall bring their own life world into the discussion and that we try to open up to understanding the normativity of others. Empirical work is no foreigner in theological and ethical scholarship. It is a friend, helping scholars to avoid becoming "resistant" to empirical material and insights.

Normativity and empirical data in practical theology

Harald Hegstad

Practical theology is the theological discipline most explicitly dedicated to "practice". This practice might be understood in different ways. Traditionally, practical theology has primarily been related to the practice of the pastor and other professionals in the church. In a broader ecclesiological perspective this understanding of practice is obviously too narrow: Professional practice is a dimension of the field of practice that is represented by the church as such. At the same time it could also be argued that limiting the concept of practice to ecclesial practice is also a too narrow definition: The practice of the church cannot be understood isolated from religious and non-religious practices in the broader society.[1]

Whether the field of practice is understood in a broader or a more narrow sense, practical theology is either way linked to the church as a field of practice. This relation on the one hand defines a certain thematic field, or a range of phenomena, that is being studied by practical theology. On the other hand it constitutes a certain perspective on this field, as it works with a certain perspective "from within" the practice and self understanding of the church. This perspective does not exclude a critical perspective inherent to all scholarly research. On the contrary, a certain perspective "from within" is central to the identity of practical theology as an academic discipline.

The question of perspective is intrinsically linked to the question of normativity. In practical theology, normativity is not something external to the field studied. The perspective "from within" means that practical theology is not independent from the normativity in the field studied. At the same time, practical theology as an academic discipline should not reflect the normativity in the field uncritically, but rather engage with it in a critical manner.

Normative reflection based on a certain perspective "from within" is not something unique to (practical) theology, even if it takes different shapes in different contexts. It could be argued that all scientific activity in some sense is based on a perspective "from within", as the researcher cannot exclude herself from the reality studied. This is true of the investigation of the physical and biological reality of which the scientist is a part.

---

1 Cf. the discussion of different practical theological "paradigms" in Olav Skjevesland, *Invitasjon til praktisk teologi. En faginnføring* (Oslo: Luther, 1999).

It is also true of the researcher in humanities – as a human – studying human phenomena. It is also true of the social scientist – as a social being – studying the reality of human societies. Scientific research is in itself a human and social activity, and as such part of the reality which is studied, at least in a broader sense. This means that scientific research may never be understood isolated from its human and social context.

As such all scientific research has some sort of normative basis. On the most basic levels standards like "truth" and "objectivity" are important normative ideas for the idea of science itself. There is a general consensus that there are limits to which procedures scientists may engage in, in order not to cause harm to individuals or to the environment. Most scientists would also – sometimes in a very vague sense – understand their activity as a contribution to some sort of "common good".

As these aspects may be more easily overlooked in natural sciences, they are more obvious in the social sciences. Some social scientists have a more general idea of the humanizing effects of their research. Others have more specific ideas of how their research is contributing to more defined ends like "liberation", "giving voice to the voiceless", etc. In some instances this type of normative interests are tied to the interests of a certain group, e.g. underprivileged people. It is less accepted in the research community to link normative interests to the good of established institutions and elites, even if this does not prohibit it from happening. Criticism of science for serving institutional interests is also a normative perspective on science.

An important aspect of scientific normativity is that it is not hidden and implied, but explicit and open for discussion and criticism. This both applies to research that strives to be value free, and for research that has a declared normative basis. Research turning into ideology or the use of science for pure institutional legitimization should be criticized.

Normativity and professional practice

Normative questions related to Practical Theology are not only linked to the question of scientific normativity in general, but also imply questions of normativity related to studying a certain field of practice, in order to evaluate and improve practice in that given field. This is not a unique role for practical theology, as it shares it with other practice-oriented academic disciplines. Medicine is e.g. not just a branch of descriptive human biology, but investigates and evaluates the practice of medical professionals. The explicit and implicit normativity obviously lies in human health and well being. Nursing science is a field closely related to medicine, even if it is different as nurses have different tasks from doctors. In both cases, "best practice", seems to be a norm that is established trough research and education.

The field of pedagogic investigates phenomena like learning and formation, and how this happens through the practice of teachers and other agents for learning. Other disciplines connected to professional practice have similar perspectives, e.g. psychology and law. In all these disciplines questions of normativity are not only connected to the general context of the research, such questions are rather related to the concrete practices conducted in a given field, in particular the practice of professionals. Such disciplines research professional practice, not only to describe it but also to evaluate and improve it. They develop theories of practice based on analysis of practice.

Understood as the discipline of the professional practice of the pastor, practical theology fits well into such a pattern. In the traditional European university system pastors have been educated at theological faculties, medical doctors at medical faculties, lawyers at faculties of law, etc. An understanding of practical theology as the discipline studying the practice of the church in a broader sense is not very different from the development in other professional disciplines, which also focus on the role of the professional in wider fields of practice (the health system, the legal field etc.). In terms of normativity, the norms guiding the practice of the professional have to be in accordance with (or at least not in contradiction to) the norms regulating the field of practice.

Normativity in a theological context

In the preceding I have pointed to the fact that the question of normativity in a general sense is a theme practical theology shares with other academic disciplines and sciences. In a more specific sense practical theology shares questions of normativity with other disciplines of practice. Much of what could be discussed in the context of an article such as this is shared with these other contexts. In the following, I will focus on the specific meaning of normativity within practical theology. An important question in this context is what characterizes practical theology as a *theological* discipline. This is on the one hand a question regarding the relation between theology and other academic fields, on the other hand a question regarding the relation between practical theology and other theological sub-disciplines.

As indicated in the introduction of this article I understand practical theology to represent a sort of perspective "from within" in the practice field of the church. A similar understanding could be applied to theology as such; as a reflection not only of the practice of the church, but also the beliefs, values and understandings connected to it. Traditionally, systematic theology has been the theological sub-discipline assigned to the analysis of the cognitive content of Christian faith. This activity is qualified as theological by taking a perspective "from within", analyzing this content from the assumption that this perspective may represent a valid interpretation of reality.

In his classical definition Karl Barth defines Christian dogmatics as a theological discipline in the following way: "As a theological discipline dogmatics is the scientific self-examination of the Christian Church with respect to the content of its distinctive talk about God."[2] On the one hand Barth points to the perspective "from within": Theology is done on behalf of the church, investigating the content of its faith and doctrine. On the other hand Barth points to a critical perspective by his use of the expression "scientific self-examination". Theology is not simply reproduction and defence of what the church thinks and does, it is also a critical enterprise. The criterion for such criticism is for Barth given in the *object* of theology: God.[3]

The problem with studying God is of course that God is not an empirical object given as a direct object of experience. Instead theology has to study human religious experiences, talk and actions and the contexts of these. The empirical material for theology is thus not different from what is available to other disciplines; it is only studying it from a different perspective, in the light of the Christian belief in God. When theology investigates religious experiences, they are analyzed as possible experiences of God. When theology analyses utterances about God, a central issue is whether such utterances can be understood as true speech about God or

---

2 Karl Barth, *Church Dogmatics. Vol I: The Doctrine of the word of God*, Part one (Edinburgh: T&T Clark, 1975)., p. 3.
3 Cf. Jan-Olav Henriksen's understanding of theology as "conscience and self criticism" of the church, Jan-Olav Henriksen, *Teologi i dag. Samvittighet og selvkritikk* (Bergen: Fagbokforlaget, 2007).

not. When theology talks about reality as such, it understands it as if it is created by God, and asks what consequences such a presupposition may have for the understanding of the world as it is empirically available.

Wolfhart Pannenberg has convincingly argued that belief in God in the terms of theory of science should be understood in the category of a hypothesis. Theology takes the truth of this belief as its point of departure, however, this does not exclude theology from testing and questioning this presupposition. The critical character of theology does not only include the details, but also the foundations.[4]

The understanding of theology as representing a perspective "from within", raises the question of how to identify this "within". Understanding Christian theology as talking from within the Christian tradition as such is problematic, as this tradition only exists in and through particular historical versions of this tradition. A theological perspective "from within" will necessarily be positioned within a particular version of the tradition. In this sense theology has to be "confessional" in some sense or another.[5] This does not exclude en ecumenical perspective; however, such a perspective needs some sort of grounding in a given tradition. Such "grounding" does of course not mean an uncritical relation to the given tradition, rather an obligation to discuss aspects of the tradition from a critical perspective.

Christian traditions only exist in and through social groups and organisation. Theology's perspective "from within" also implies a relation to Christian churches. This is implied in Barth's understanding of theology when he understands dogmatics as the "scientific self-examination of the Christian Church". This does not mean that theology is simply a tool for church institutions and church leaders. Even if theology should be accountable to the church, as an academic discipline it also needs independence and critical distance. At the same time, the relation to the church is not only a relation to the church as an institution, but rather to the church as a community of people. As an analogy to social scientists wanting to give voice to the voiceless in society, theology should listen to and give voice to ordinary people in the Christian community.

---

4   Wolfhart Pannenberg, *Theology and the philosophy of science* (London: Darton Longman & Todd, 1976), pp. 326–345.
5   Cf Harald Hegstad, "Fra konfesjonalisme til differensiert konsensus. Refleksjoner om luthersk teologi i en økumenisk kontekst," in *Kirkens bekjennelse i historisk og aktuelt perspektiv*. Festskrift til Kjell Olav Sannes, ed. Lars Østnor, Torleiv Austad, and Tormod Engelsviken (Trondheim: Tapir akademisk, 2010).

When theology is (critically) interpreting the church's faith in God, it does so with respect to the object of this faith, i.e. God. This mean that theology is not primarily about belief in God or about religious consciousness, it is asking about God. For Christian theology the understanding of God relates to the life and words of Jesus, as this is testified and interpreted in the New Testament – on the background of the understanding of God in the Old Testament. This assigns a special normative status to the biblical writings in the understanding of God in his relation to the world. This relation does not only belong to the past, but also to the present and the future. Christian theology of God does not primarily refer to timeless truths of God's being, but rather to God as he is acting in the world. In the perspective of normativity, one may say that these acts of God have a normative aspect: From the perspective of the biblical message, responding to God's acts in an adequate way, even participating in these acts, seems to be something believers and the community of believers should strive to do. This means that normativity in a theological perspective can't be reduced to a question of what "ought to be the case" – the question of normativity is embedded in the understanding of reality as such.

A critical, normatively based, question for practical theology analyzing the practice of the church would then be whether this practice can be understood as participating in God's acts in and for the world. A text book definition of practical theology that seems to be in line what this, is given by John Swinton and Harriet Mowat: "Practical Theology is critical, theological reflection on the practices of the Church as they interact with the practices of the world, with a view to ensuring and enabling faithful participation in God's redemptive practices in, to and for the world."[6] From a Lutheran perspective one could argue for adding "God's *creative and* redemptive practices...", indicating that God is acting with the world in a twofold way, through creation and redemption. God is acting not only through the church, but also through the world.

This also means that the question of normativity in theology is not only a question of "norms" and "values", strictly separated from statements on how things "are" (cf. Hume). Understanding God's acts as normative, implies that the question of normativity is also linked to the understanding of reality, including the understanding of God and the understanding of how God acts in the world. Such a perspective should not lead to easy answers in normative questions, as theology has no direct knowledge of

---

6   John Swinton and Harriet Mowat, *Practical theology and qualitative research* (London: SCM Press, 2006), p. 6.

God's concrete acts, as these are never "pure", but happen under given historical and social conditions. The understanding of God's acts is thus an interpretative task that includes historical, social and theological dimensions.

An influential contribution to the understanding of practical theology in the wider context of theology has been proposed by Don S. Browning in his book *A Fundamental Practical Theology*.[7] Understanding the theological project as essentially practical, he distinguishes between four movements in the theological enterprise: descriptive theology, historical theology, systematic theology and strategic practical theology. The merit of this model is twofold: It attempts to keep the different theological disciplines together in a comprehensive understanding of theology, and it proposes a way of relating practice and theory to each other. Theology is not understood as theory divided from practice, but as reflection built on practice, and related to practice. It starts from practice and returns to practice. It starts with the descriptive movement to describe and interpret empirical realities. This descriptive work then leads to theological questions that have to be worked on in the light of Christian history, tradition and doctrine. In historical theology questions from practice are related to central texts and events of the Christian faith, including the biblical texts. In systematic theology a critical and philosophical perspective is added to the questions, discussing normativity and the validity of truth claims.[8]

Building on the accomplishments of the three first phases, strategic practical theology "brings the general fruits of descriptive theology and practically oriented historical and systematic theology back into contact with the concrete situation of action".[9] It asks the question of what means, strategies and rhetoric that should be used in a concrete situation. Contrary to the traditional view, this phase of practical theology is not to be understood as an application to practice of theology as a theoretical discipline, but rather "the culmination of an inquiry that has been practical throughout".[10]

An important element in Browning's model is that it includes what he calls "descriptive theology" in the different movements of theological research and reflection, not only as a part of practical theology, but as the-

---

7 Don S. Browning, *A fundamental practical theology. Descriptive and strategic proposals* (Minneapolis: Fortress Press, 1991).
8 Ibid., pp. 47–54.
9 Ibid., p. 55.
10 Ibid., p. 57.

ology as such. The descriptive movement of theology is thus also linked to systematic theology. This makes empirical research an integrated part of theology, and thus links normative theological questions to empirical data.

Integration of empirical methods in theological research also creates a closer link between theology and the social sciences. In not too distant a past the question of the relation between theology and the empirical field was identified with the relation between theology and the social sciences. Until the 1980's the main question usually was whether and in what way theology could learn from the social sciences and in what way social scientific data and results could be useful for theology. From this time theologians, especially practical theologians, argued that empirical research should be a part of the theological enterprise itself. An important author in this context was the Dutch theologian, Johannes A. van der Ven. Instead of just learning from the social sciences, he argued that theology should include the empirical approach in its own methodological repertoire. His concept of "empirical theology" fits very well into Browning's concept of "descriptive theology" as a basic theological movement.[11]

The use of an empirical approach within theology raises the question of how this appraoch is integrated in theology, and how it is related to other academic disciplines. Van der Ven here distinguishes between three models, the models of monodisciplinarity, multidisciplinarity, interdisciplinarity and intradisciplinarity. While in the monodisciplinary model of theology relates directly to praxis, without the use of scientific methods, in the multidisciplinary model the social scientists offers the empirical description and analysis and the theologian subsequently develops a theological reflection. The interdisciplinary model then adds an element of cooperation and interaction between social scientists and theologians. In the intradisciplinary model advocated by van der Ven himself, theology takes up the empirical methods and techniques developed within other social sciences and makes use of them within its own work. This is in principle not different from what theology has done in other areas throughout history, when including e.g. methods and perspectives from historical science, philosophy, literary criticism and so forth.[12] This means that a theologian working in this field should himself master empirical methods and social scientific perspectives! This does not exclude the necessity for

---

11 Johannes A. van der Ven, *Practical Theology. An Empirical Approach* (Kampen: Kok, 1993).
12 Ibid., pp. 89ff.

interdisciplinary collaboration with social scientists who are not themselves theologians: theology should make use of insights and results from the general social sciences, and follow the same methodological standards in its own work.

The growing number of theologians utilizing empirical methodology is a clear indication that what van der Ven names as the model of intradisciplinarity in a rather short time has been tested and accepted as a viable approach within theology. The experience from my own institution confirms this: Until the mid 1990's empirical projects within theological research were very rare, today they are one of the main methodological approaches used in theological research, including research on churches and congregations. This rather rapid acceptance of empirical approaches within theological research also means that this is a rather immature field, with basic questions yet to be discussed and clarified. Among these is clearly the question of normativity. On the one hand the question is how to deal with normativity related to empirical data. On the other hand the question is about the relation between theological normativity and normativity in other disciplines, including the social sciences.

As a comment to this second question it is necessary to point to the fact that even if theology represents its own type of discourse, with its own type of embedded normativity, it is not completely separated from the discourse of normativity in other academic disciplines, e.g. the social sciences. I say this in opposition to theologians like John Milbank, who understand modern social theory as a secular alternative to the Christian and theological narrative.[13] Even if we have to respect the differences between theology and the social sciences, they should not be isolated from each other, even when it comes to normative questions. Social scientific questions about e.g. "communicative action" (Habermas) do not necessarily stand in contrast to the theological question of God's will for society, even if they may be different, and even if they have their specific agenda, theologians should engage in the general academic discussion, and they should learn from other disciplines for their own work.

---

13 John Milbank, *Theology and social theory. Beyond secular reason* (Cambridge, Mass.: Blackwell, 1991).

Normativity in the empirical field

A possible weakness in Browning's model of theology, identified by R. Ganzevoort, is a tendency to separate the descriptive and empirical phase, taken care of by practical theology, and the theoretical and normative phase, taken care of by systematic theology. In some sense normativity in such an understanding is "added" to the empirical field by systematic theological reflection. As Ganzevoort points out, normativity and theoretical presuppositions are already included in practice itself. When reflecting normatively on a certain practice, the normative elements which are already there, have to be taken into consideration.[14]

This is especially necessary in a practical theology that understands itself as a critical self-reflection on behalf of the church. The normative questions – and sources – that practical theology deals with are not completely different from the normativity already embedded in the practice in the field that is being studied. If so, practical theology would no longer represent a perspective "from within". This does not mean there is no difference between practice itself and the academic reflection on this practice. It is thus necessary to distinguish between first and second order discourses, first order discourses representing the discourse within the primary religious and ecclesial practice, second order discourses representing the discourse of the academic analysis of the first order discourse. These discourses follow partly different rules and interests, but they are also closely connected, especially in a theological context. The audience of the practical theologian is not only the academic community; he is also contributing to the church's own critical evaluation of its practice.[15]

Analysis of normativity in the field is thus an important contribution to connecting the normative theological discussion with what happens in the field itself. Ganzevoort puts it this way: "The analysis of the normative dimension in first (and second) order discourses is essential to overcome the seeming gap between quasi-objective empirical research and normative theological interpretation."[16]

---

14 R. Ruard Ganzevoort, "What you see is what you get. Social construction and normativity in practical theology," in *Normativity and empirical research in theology*, ed. J. A. van der Ven and Michael Scherer-Rath, Empirical studies in theology (Leiden Boston: Brill, 2004)., p. 24f.
15 Cf. ibid., p. 20–22.
16 Ibid., p. 31.

The recognition of the existence and importance of the normativity in the empirical field is not just a statement on a theoretical level; it should also have also consequences for how empirical research is conducted, making questions for the explicit and implicit values and norms in the field an important area of study. Normativity is an important empirical fact in itself, rather than something "added" to the field afterwards. According to Aad de Jong the investigation of norms that guide the field studies has been nearly overlooked in practical theological research so far. He maintains that a broader engagement in empirical normativity would give an important contribution both to the empirical understanding of the field as well as to the normative reflections on the hand of the practical theologian.[17]

From a theological point of view theological normativity is especially important to investigate: How do people understand their lives and actions in light of their belief or non-belief in God? Of course theological normativity in a second order sense cannot simply be extracted from an analysis of the normativity in the field, as it has to be critically examined on a critical and academic level. The sources for such a normative evaluation are in principle none other than the normative sources for the church's understanding of God and his acts in the world. The fact that these sources (Scripture, tradition, experience, etc.) are understood differently in different ecclesial traditions corresponds to the unavoidable confessional character of theology (cf. above).

The close connection between normativity in first and second order discourse means that the importance of normativity in the first order discourse is not limited to practical theology. No systematic theological normative reflection should take place independently from references to the empirical context of this reflection. Most systematicians would agree that systematic theology needs to take human experience into consideration, especially th experience that characterizes the context the systematician operates within. Too often the understanding of the context has had no real empirical foundation, but has rather been built upon personal or anecdotal experience, or mere assumptions. In order to secure its academic standards systematic theology has to establish its understanding of its context in a methodologically secured way. An empirically based understanding of the context is necessary for the validity of the theological re-

---

17 Aad de Jong, "Normative explanation in practical theology," in *Normativity and empirical research in theology*, ed. J. A. van der Ven and Michael Scherer-Rath, Empirical studies in theology (Leiden Boston: Brill, 2004).

flection. Using existing empirical research – or engaging in empirical research oneself – may contribute to better understanding and clarity.

To illustrate this last point I would like to give an example from my own research, within the field of ecclesiology in a Norwegian context. In an ethnographic study of three local parishes I investigated the relation between the church as a religious majority institution in the local society (holding a majority of the population as members) and a minority community of active participants.[18] On the one hand the study aimed at understanding the relation between these social forms of church as a sociological phenomenon: What is the relation and interaction between these two phenomena? On the other hand the study raised certain theological questions: How should this situation be interpreted from an ecclesiological point of view? Which of these social forms represents the church in a theological sense – or maybe both do? Besides a systematic-theological discussion this study also led to practical theological reflections on strategies for congregational development in contexts that were described by the study.

Normativity in strategic practical theology

In Browning's understanding of the different movements in the theological cycle practical theology is so to say placed at the beginning and at the end of the cycle. At the start of the cycle he places practical theology as "descriptive theology", as the empirical analysis of existing ecclesial practice. At the end of the cycle he places what he understands to be practical theology in its *real* sense, namely "strategic practical theology". On the basis of empirical analysis and theoretical reflection, strategic practical theology asks *what should be* the practice in the given situation, and what means and strategies could be used (Browning 55f).

This moves the question of normativity one step further: The question is not only how to understand and analyse the normativity present in the field, nor how to evaluate this normativity on the basis of theoretical and theological insights, but is also a question of how practical theology may

---

18 Harald Hegstad, *Folkekirke og trosfellesskap. Et kirkesosiologisk og ekklesiologisk grunnproblem belyst gjennom en undersøkelse av tre norske lokalmenigheter*, KIFO perspektiv nr 1 (Trondheim: Tapir, 1996), Harald Hegstad, "A minority within the majority. On the relation between the church as folk church and as a community of believers.," *Studia theologica 53* (1999).

influence the practice in the field, having a normative function. While practical theology and ecclesial practice are related to each other, it is at the same time necessary to distinguish the two from each other. It is thus necessary to distinguish between ecclesial practice in its primary sense and practical theology as theory of ecclesial practice (and as such of course a practice in itself, but on a secondary level). As pointed out by Johannes van der Ven, practical theology is not primarily involved with "concrete forms of praxis in concrete situations of concrete people, but rather in classes of praxis in classes of situations of classes of people".[19] The normative task of practical theology as an academic discipline is not to regulate concrete practice, but rather to give general rules and recommendations for categories of practices. The decision in such cases has to be made by the reflective practitioner himself, or by the group or community of practitioners. Practical theology is a contributor to normative reflection, not a judge of concrete practice. In the concrete situation a decision cannot be made just on the basis of theoretical consideration alone, it also demands a certain practical wisdom and a sense for the uniqueness of the situation.

This also means that the relation between practical theology as an academic discipline and the field of ecclesial practice should have a dialogical and discursive character. Practical theology conducts its influence not by prescribing concrete solutions, but rather through offering plausible theoretical interpretations of empirical phenomena, giving frames for understanding, and pointing to alternatives. The decision of how to use these perspectives and frames for understanding should be left to the practitioner.

Good examples of this approach are sub disciplines in practical theology like homiletics, liturgical studies and pastoral care. As basic disciplines for pastoral education and training they provide general knowledge of the field together with normative frameworks of interpretation and understanding. In this way the disciplines influence the practice of future and present pastors, without prescribing the concrete practice in detail. A weakness in these traditional fields of practical theology has been a rather weak basis in empirical knowledge and research. This means that the normative structure of these disciplines in some instances has rather been

---

19 Johannes A. van der Ven, "An empirical or a normative approach to practical-theological research? A false dilemma," in *Normativity and empirical research in theology*, ed. J. A. van der Ven and Michael Scherer-Rath, Empirical studies in theology (Leiden Boston: Brill, 2004)., p. 130.

guided by theological frameworks loosely related to methodologically secured knowledge about practice. The introduction of empirical methodology in practical theology over the last decades is about to change this picture.

An alternative, or supplementary, approach for practical theological research to simply reflect on the basis of collected empirical data is to be engaged in the field through an "action research" strategy. In "action research", the researcher is actively involved in changing a situation in a desired direction. In this type of research the researcher is not only a practitioner, but utilizes his/her theoretical insights and methodological skills. An important aspect of action research is the fact that the researcher is working with the people affected by the changes. Action research is not primarily research *on* people, but *with* people. It is "a practice of participation, engaging those who might otherwise be subjects of research or recipients of interventions to a greater or less extent as inquiring co-researchers".[20]

This type of research is also used in a theological and ecclesial context, even if few projects have been labeled as such. Research on the church *with* church members fits well with an understanding of theology as something done by and for the church. An interesting ongoing project is a project called "Action Research: Church and Society" initiated by Heythrop College, University of London.[21] The project is initiating a process called "theological action research" in selected Anglican and Catholic parishes. In this process congregational experience and practice is shared and reflected upon in conversations between researchers and practitioners. These reflections are aimed at suggesting renewed action and theology. One basic characteristic of this process is that the researchers are not put in a privileged position compared to the practitioners; the process is a shared reflection and conversation process between researchers and practitioners.

Concerning the normative aspect of practical theology this means that the researchers taking part in the process do not act normatively in the way that they provide the "answers" or make decisions. The normative element is rather understood as a *framework*, represented by the *theo-*

---

20 Peter Reason and Hilary Bradbury, eds., *The SAGE Handbook of Action Research, Participative Inquiry and Practice* (London: Sage, 2008)., p. 1.
21 A preliminary report is published in Helen Cameron et al., *Talking about God in practice. Theological action research and practical theology* (London: SCM Press, 2010).

logical character of the project. By insisting that practice should be understood and interpreted theologically, the projects created a certain normative framework, even if the consequences of this framework are subject to joint reflection. Also, theology is not understood as something "added" to practice, Christian practices are in themselves bearers of theology.[22] By enabling practitioners to understand their practice from a theological perspective (which is already inherent in the practice itself), and thereby "grow in theological fluency", the project wants to contribute to renewed practice.[23]

A similar project called "Congregational development in the folk church" has been conducted at MF Norwegian School of Theology.[24] In this project, researchers have also been working together with practitioners in ten Lutheran congregations in a process of analysis and reflection. In the first phase of this project empirical data about the congregation and the local community was collected. In order to secure the reflective use of the data, practitioners were involved in the data gathering. The data was used as a basis for a reflective process in the congregation about their situation and identity. On the basis of a renewed self-understanding the congregation was invited to discuss strategies for the future.

Researchers took part in the different steps of the process. The normative element of the process was also here primarily represented by the *framing* of the process, as the practitioners were challenged to interpret their practice and their experience in an ecclesiological framework. The project did not supply a defined ecclesiology, leaving the congregations themselves to define their ecclesiology. The normative contribution of the researchers was rather to insist that theological questions should be asked, rather than giving the answers.

These two projects illustrate important aspects of the normative aspects of practical theology. What characterizes it as a theological discipline is its attempt to understand ecclesial practice in the light of the Christian belief in God. In order to understand this practice it has to work as an empirical discipline, borrowing methodological tools and theoretical perspectives from other empirical disciplines. The normative element of the discipline is expressed in its attempts to interpret and evaluate eccle-

---

22 "Practices of faithful Christian people are themselves bearers of theology; they express the contemporary living tradition of the Christian faith." Ibid., p. 51.
23 Ibid., 58f.
24 Erling Birkedal, Harald Hegstad, and Turid Skorpe Lannem, *Menighetsutvikling i folkekirken (forthcoming),* Prismet bok (Oslo: IKO-forlaget, 2011).

sial practice critically from a theological perspective. Practical theology does not aim at regulating or prescribing concrete practice, but rather to provide theoretical frameworks and patterns for understanding. When engaging directly with practitioners in the field, this should be done in a discursive mode.

References:

Barth, Karl. *Church Dogmatics. Vol I: The Doctrine of the word of God, Part one.* Edinburgh: T&T Clark, 1975.
Birkedal, Erling, Harald Hegstad, and Turid Skorpe Lannem. *Menighetsutvikling i folkekirken* (forthcoming), Prismet bok. Oslo: IKO-forlaget, 2011.
Browning, Don S. *A fundamental practical theology. Descriptive and strategic proposals.* Minneapolis: Fortress Press, 1991.
Cameron, Helen, Deborah Bhatti, Catherine Duce, James Sweeney, and Clare Watkins. *Talking about God in practice. Theological action research and practical theology.* London: SCM Press, 2010.
de Jong, Aad. "Normative explanation in practical theology." In *Normativity and empirical research in theology*, edited by J. A. van der Ven and Michael Scherer-Rath, 35-58. Leiden Boston: Brill, 2004.
Ganzevoort, R. Ruard. "What you see is what you get. Social construction and normativity in practical theology." In *Normativity and empirical research in theology*, edited by J. A. van der Ven and Michael Scherer-Rath, 17-33. Leiden Boston: Brill, 2004.
Hegstad, Harald. *Folkekirke og trosfellesskap. Et kirkesosiologisk og ekklesiologisk grunnproblem belyst gjennom en undersøkelse av tre norske lokalmenigheter*, KIFO perspektiv nr 1. Trondheim: Tapir, 1996.
Hegstad, Harald. "Fra konfesjonalisme til differensiert konsensus. Refleksjoner om luthersk teologi i en økumenisk kontekst." In *Kirkens bekjennelse i historisk og aktuelt perspektiv. Festskrift til Kjell Olav Sannes,* edited by Lars Østnor, Torleiv Austad and Tormod Engelsviken, 199-209. Trondheim: Tapir akademisk, 2010.
Hegstad, Harald. "A minority within the majority. On the relation between the church as folk church and as a community of believers." *Studia theologica 53* (1999): 119-31.
Henriksen, Jan-Olav. *Teologi i dag. Samvittighet og selvkritikk.* Bergen: Fagbokforlaget, 2007.
Milbank, John. *Theology and social theory : beyond secular reason*, Signposts in theology. Cambridge, Mass.: Blackwell, 1991.
Pannenberg, Wolfhart. *Theology and the philosophy of science.* London: Darton Longman & Todd, 1976.
Reason, Peter, and Hilary Bradbury, eds. *The SAGE Handbook of Action Research, Participative Inquiry and Practice.* London: Sage, 2008.
Skjevesland, Olav. *Invitasjon til praktisk teologi. En faginnføring.* Oslo: Luther, 1999.

Swinton, John, and Harriet Mowat. Practical theology and qualitative research. London: SCM Press, 2006.

van der Ven, Johannes A. "An empirical or a normative approach to practical-theological research? A false dilemma." In *Normativity and empirical research in theology,* edited by J. A. van der Ven and Michael Scherer-Rath, 101-35. Leiden Boston: Brill, 2004.

van der Ven, Johannes A. *Practical Theology. An Empirical Approach.* Kampen: Kok, 1993.

The non-confessional study of religion and its normative dimensions

Ingvild Sælid Gilhus

> One of the first things that I learnt when I started teaching within a department of religious studies (and indeed one of the first things I and others teach new and prospective students) is that the study of religion is different from theology. The establishment of the discipline – certainly within European context, and still to a large extent in North America – has been fought with Christian theology as the significant other: the maxim is that the study of religion is not the same as the doing of theology.
>
> (Malory Nye 2000: 450)

The non-confessional study of religion – whether it is called comparative religion, history of religions, religious studies, science of religion or simply the study of religion – was created and continues to exist with theology as its significant other. This position has carried with it normative implications from the beginning. Some of these norms are explicit, while others are implicit.

In this article I will discuss the norms of the non-confessional study of religion. I will do so by giving a short survey of its different research-paradigms; discuss its relationship to theology; see how the category of religion is shaped and used in non-confessional academic practice; and ask what happens when a two-field approach to religion, where the praxis of religion and the study of religion are placed in different fields, is challenged and exchanged for a one-field approach. My own point of reference is the non-confessional study of religion in Scandinavia, which is sometimes placed in theological faculties and sometimes in faculties of arts and/or humanities.

The study of religion and its research paradigms

The secular study of religion was from the beginning constituted as different from theology. Its subject is on principle the study of *all* religions, not only Christianity, and *all forms* of religion, not only the religion of the theologians and the elite. There are some explicit norms. Chief among them are a comparative approach and the ideal of being neutral. Both these norms were present in the formative phase and both are connected to him who is usually counted as the founding father of the non-confessional study of religion, Friedrich Max Müller.

Müller saw the value of religion, but preferred its constitutive phase: "Whenever we can trace back a religion to its first beginnings, we find it free from many of the blemishes that offend us in its later phases" (*Chips from a German Workshop* 1867: xxiii). He was himself a pious Christian and characterized Christianity as "das gelobtes Land" in relation to other religions (Klimkeit 1997:37). All the same, in his *Introduction to a Science of Religion* (1873) Müller presents the ideal of neutrality in the study of religion and was also a strong advocate of the comparative approach of this new science, which he called comparative religion. His comment to the famous theologian of his days, Adolf van Harnack, is often quoted and has forever after functioned as a slogan for the comparative approach and as a demarcation towards theology: "He who knows one, knows none".

James Frazer (1854-1941) also stressed the comparative dimension, a fact that is reflected in the title of the first edition of his *magnum opus*: *The Golden Bough. A Study in Comparative Religion* (1890). Frazer thought that humans went through three stages: from magic, to religion and finally to science.

Several of the adherents of the evolutionist paradigm were bent on giving religion a non-religious explanation and were what has sometimes been called reductionists. It means that they explained religion by means of non-religious factors and as an epiphenomenon to more fundamental phenomena. In other words, they explained it away. Most famous among them are the sociologist Émile Durkheim and the psychoanalyst Sigmund Freud who described religion as an illusion.

In opposition to many of the evolutionists the adherents of the phenomenological approach based themselves on empathy towards religion and saw it as a *sui generis* phenomenon, something that had an essence. According to the phenomenological paradigm, the believers were always right. This was, for instance, claimed by Wilhelm Brede Kristensen (1867-1953), professor in the history of religion in Leiden. Mircea Eliade (1907-1986), professor in Chicago, believed in the existence of a religious transcendence and in religious archetypes. He saw man as a *homo religiosus*, which means that according to him human beings have an inborn capacity for religion.

The friendliness of phenomenology towards religion was usually obtained at some costs. It was, for instance, easier to subscribe to the view that the believers were completely right in the early days when the study of religions in the main consisted of a study of religious texts from the past, and not for instance, of religious conflicts in the present, and it was easier to claim that religion had a uniquely positive value when the significance of sex, power and social class was in the main overlooked. In both the older paradigms – the evolutionistic and the phenomenological – scholars were critical towards popular religion and towards religion that had deviated too much from the formative phase of the canonical texts. Religion was usually seen as more valuable when belonging to an elite, mostly priests, than when it took the form of, for instance, magic.

Today a non-confessional study of religion evolves in the main within what could be called a cultural paradigm. According to this paradigm, religion – similar to culture in general – is seen as the product of social constructions, and as created by humans. The cultural study of religion is often connected to a suspension of value judgements when it comes to the truth/lack of truths of religions. This approach is sometimes designated "methodological atheism" (Berger 1967), or more fittingly as "methodological agnosticism" (Smart 1973).

Cognitive studies have become a strong and innovative branch within the study of religion using cognitivist, evolutionary or neuropsychological perspectives. Within this branch there has been a focus on how humans are "programmed" to develop and sustain beliefs in superhuman beings. In the words of Aaron W. Hughes, one gets the impression that thinking about the origins and persistence of religion "has largely migrated out of the humanities into the natural and behavioural sciences, even if such theorizing is still largely carried out in Religious Studies departments." (Hughes 2010:294). Cognitive studies of religion aim at explaining (away) religion.

This short survey of research paradigms reveals a complex and ambiguous picture of norms and values in the non-confessional study of religion. Neutrality and comparison are part of it, though how these norms have been acted out has varied. The insider/outsider problem has received different solutions with an explanatory approach in the evolutionistic and the cognitive paradigms; an empathic approach in the phenomenological paradigm; while in the cultural paradigm there has been a strong tendency to promote methodological agnosticism. Here scholars describe religion as part of human communication and as a social construction (for instance Jensen 2003).

Though each of these paradigms has pulled scholars in certain directions, the norms of the individual scholars have varied and vary. Max Müller cherished religion, while Freud considered religion to be an illusion.

Comparison is not always paired with neutrality, but sometimes goes together with hierarchy and with a ranking of religions and types of religion. One example is magic, which until the 1990s was usually kept outside the category of religion and looked down upon. Another example is world-religions. Buddhism has frequently been treated more positively than the so-called "law-religions", as Sigurd Hjelde has pointed out, using Trevor Ling's *History of Religion East and West* (1968) as an example (Hjelde 2001).

Theology and the non-confessional study of religion

While scholars of religion try to make a division between religion and the study of religion, theology is committed to its religious fundamentals. It varies what theologians and theological faculties count as fundamentals – a conservative theologian/theological faculty has more fundamentals to defend than a liberal theologian/theological faculty. In all cases, however, canonical texts – the Bible – function as *norma normans*, the norming norm. In the non-confessional study of religion the norms, or shared values, are not rooted in canonical texts, instead they are rooted in an historical past (Max Müller et al.); in the Enlightenment narrative about the division between religion and science; and in the continuous struggle to be different from theology.

The relationship between theology and the study of religion is sometimes difficult, partly due to the different norms of the two professions, partly due to fight about limited resources at the universities, and partly due to the struggle to maintain the difference between them. (The non-confessional study of religion has from the beginning often been accommodated in theological faculties). However, the fronts are usually not as sharp as they were when the Norwegian scholar of religion, Wilhelm Schencke, argued that the Theological Faculty at the University of Oslo should be closed and characterized it as the inflamed appendix of the university, because of its commitments to theological values and norms (*Tidens Tegn* 1913). He got a professorship in the history of religions the year after, and was moved from the Theological faculty to the Faculty of Arts.

In spite of a certain antagonism, there are also collaborations and joint research projects between scholars of religion and theologians, mostly in the historical disciplines of the Old Testament, New Testament and Church History. In these disciplines historical interests tend to unite the scholars in theology and the study of religion and the differences between theology and the non-confessional study of religion do not seem to matter so much.

It is always implicit in the non-confessional study of religion that there exists an alternative study of religion – theology – that is not comparative and neutral in the same way as the non-confessional study of religion purports to be. The struggle to be something different from theology has, however, never been completely successful. One example is that the study of Christianity took place solely within a theological context, another example is the construction of and use of terminology.

Part of the dividing line between theology and the study of religion was in the earlier days, (and is somewhere still the norm, for instance in Sweden), that Christianity was studied in the theological/Christianity departments and was not part of the curriculum of the non-confessional study of religion. This divide was explained as a division of work – the subject of theologians was Christianity, while the subject of the scholars of religion was everything else that counted as religion, in the older days described as "foreign religions". This had as a consequence that Christianity was seen as something special and not regarded as religion on line with the other religions. Taking into consideration that the non-confessional study of religion is basically a comparative study, the exclusion of Christianity is/was peculiar. Excluding Christianity from the comparative study of religion is as if one of the main branches of language, for instance Indo-European languages, was excluded from the study of linguistics.

The antagonism that is sometimes present between theology and the non-confessional study of religion does not mean that Christianity/theology has not influenced the study of religion. A main part of the curriculum in the study of religion is world religions, a category that has been created after the model of Christianity (Masuzawa 2005) and with categories that are dependent on Christianity.

Concepts are always part of the constitutive normativity of all sciences. When, for instance, segments of religion in the contemporary Western world are called 'new religion', 'New Age', 'spirituality' or 'alternative religion', it implies that religion is seen from a perspective of normative religion, religious power and established institutions, *i.e.* Christianity, and to a minor degree seen more neutrally as living practices and beliefs among people (Sutcliffe 2006, Stringer 2008, Woodhead 2010). Other times neutrality has won through. The concept of "Muhammedanism" is long gone, and so are also concepts like "primitive religion" and "witch doctors" (Donovan 1990: 107-108).

The non-confessional study of religion in the university and the exclusion of religion

What is the nodal point of the study of religion? In this article it has been suggested that its relationship to theology is constitutive for the secular study of religion and in some ways also determinative for the norms of this study.

Birgitte Schepelern Johansen has recently analyzed the communication between students and teachers in the departments for the Study of Religion in two Danish universities, the University of Aarhus and the University of Copenhagen (Johansen 2010). She points out that the establishment of a science of religion took place parallel to the construction of the modern category of religion, distinct from, for instance, politics and science.

One of Johansen's questions is how religion as a specific category was established in concrete practice (Johansen 2010:11). Johansen claims that her research offers an answer to Talal Asad's question: "What might an anthropology of the secular look like?" (Johansen 2010:10). Her dissertation illuminates the norms and ideas which prevail in academic-didactic practice as well as the implicit and explicit criticism of religion that is transmitted in these milieus. Her aim is to see how the category of religion is constructed in an empirical field. The analysis is based on observation of teaching, interviews with teachers and students and, to a small extent, on literature read by the students. Her thesis is that these departments for the study of religion could be regarded as places where the secular category of religion is produced and thus they contribute to uphold the secular separation between the state and religion.

Johansen shows how the professional circles in the study of religion establish the differences between the empirically accessible and the metaphysical, focus more on religious praxis than on religious ideas and distance themselves from the Protestant conception of religion. Johansen analyses, for instance, metaphors and jokes that contribute to establish a zone free from religion – the place where a study of religion according to the departments under scrutiny ideally should be. According to her the basic dividing line in the study of religion – a line that teachers and students struggle to create and maintain – is the distinction between religion and the study of religion. The goal is to create a neutral space, free of religious practice, where religion may be studied in a secular way.

The distinction between science and religion is a nodal point in the teaching, because the distinction is frequently made and triggers off engagement, and because violations of the distinction are immediately sanctioned (Johansen 2010:255). The narrative about the progress of science and its breaking away from religion functions as a founding myth and a paradigmatic story for the secular study of religion.

Part of the teaching consists in what Johansen aptly calls "levelling" (*nivellering*) which implies that the teachers try to counterbalance the established differences between religions by being more critical towards some religions and branches of religion than towards others. The levelling usually means to normalize a phenomenon, a group or an action that others (who are not students or scholars of religion), find to be deviant or abnormal (Johansen 2010:258).

Whose side are we on? (Becker 1967) I suggest that the struggle to establish a new balance in the field of religions – the levelling activity – makes opposition in itself into a special norm. The study of religion is, for instance, usually on the side of religions and branches of religion that have got run over by church history, the so-called heretics, and sometimes, but not always, also on the side of new religious movements and those religions of modernity that frequently receive a bad press coverage in the contemporary world (Beckford and Richardson 2007: 407).

The Norwegian social scientist Rune Slagstad has launched the fruitful concept "oppositional science" (*opposisjonsvitenskap*) (Slagstad 1998; Slagstad 2009). According to Slagstad, an oppositional science aims at seeing society from the perspective of those who are governed and/or are on the margins of society. Examples of opposition sciences from the 1970s are sociology, educational science, criminology and the study of sex and gender. The non-confessional study of religion is not an opposition science in quite the same way as the examples just mentioned, because these sciences have been more intent on contributing to making actual reforms in society and have succeeded in doing so more than the study of religion has ever done. However, the implicit critical view of the ruling religion (Christianity) and the positive interest in religions and form of religions that are usually seen as marginal, for instance Christian heretical movements and new religious movements, show that the study of religion has some similarities to an opposition science. It also shows that the value of being neutral is sometimes overrun.

Opposition within the non-confessional study of religion sometimes also implies criticism of religion in itself and thus challenges the ideal of neutrality even further. This critical position has some adherents, also in Scandinavia, but it is seen most clearly in the USA where the conflict between religious studies of religion and non-confessional studies of religion is sharp and articulated. Russell T. McCutcheon is one example of a scholar who promotes a type of oppositional thinking about religion which implies debunking religion and unveiling religious claims as untrue. Scholars should, according to McCutcheon and according to the title of one of his books, be "critics not caretakers" of religion (McCutcheon 2001).

McCutcheon's position has in its turn been heavily criticised by other scholars, most prominently by Donald Wiebe. Wiebe finds McCutcheon "no more concerned for a purely scientific study of religion than are the religiously and theologically oriented students in the field whom he opposes." (Wiebe 2005: 29). Wiebe sees it as another variety of an ideological position, where religious is exchanged for non-religious. According to Wiebe, the scholar of religion should participate in the public sphere *qua* scholar and "limit herself/himself to descriptive and explanatory accounts of how religious institutions, insight, and commitment actually play out in various societies but without normative comment about these matters in the public domain." (Wiebe 2005:26). Wiebe has several times criticized the American Academy of Religion for promoting a religious agenda (for instance Wiebe 2006). In other words, Wiebe fiercely defends an agnostic approach and the value of being neutral.

Neutrality is not a self-explaining term. According to Peter Donovan it is not an observer-neutrality or a participant-neutrality that is aimed at in the study of religion, but a role-neutrality, more like that which is expected of a judge in court. This type of neutrality includes the use of non-prejudicial language and the suspension of belief and disbelief (Donovan 1990).

Two-field science meets postmodernism

The wish to cleanse the study of religion of the practice of religion and distinguish sharply between religion and science, contributes to establishing two distinct fields. In this two-field approach, scholars of religion have a tendency to rank the study of religion higher than religion (Gilhus 2009: 27ff; Johansen 2010). All forms of religion are measured against a universal non-religious category of religion. Johansen points out that the history of religions and the sociology of religion promote scientific ideals that to a certain point are formed by modernity (Johansen 2010:110): "Through these ways of shaping and relating to the categories as something mutually exclusive, the academic practice at the departments promotes ideals of science and notions of religion that have quite a modernistic ring to it – something that points towards the context of origin for the study." (Johansen 2010:284).

What will happen if the study of religion is reinstalled in a postmodern context? What will, for instance, happen to the insider/outsider problem? André Droogers discusses the second question in an article called "As Close as a Scholar Can Get. Exploring a One-Field Approach to the Study of Religion" (Droogers 2008). His point of departure is that religion is a relatively new category, formed as the opposite of science, and that metaphysical causes are not accepted in the study of religion:

> The delicate relationship between religious studies and its object creates a methodological problem that other disciplines need not face. If the scholar's task is to study empirically a field whose defining part cannot be verified empirically or is even denied reality, special caution is necessary. One must then ask whether the accepted asymmetry between science and religion may not hamper scholarly understanding (Droogers 2008: 448).

Droogers' answer to this question is to investigate the possibility of establishing a one-field perspective *á la* an anthropological fieldwork where the scholars and the believers are put on the same level. He adds that since science, including the study of religion, contributes to diminish religion in a society, it shows that religion and the study of religion are in the same field.

In the holistic and contextualized approach of anthropology the researcher tries as much as possible to be part of what he/she studies. However, Droogers sees the paradox in that the researcher participates wholeheartedly in the fieldwork, but writes about it afterwards on scientific premises. One could say that during the anthropological process of research a one-field approach is followed by a two-field approach.

Droogers recommends a playful attitude to one's object of research. Instead of the methodological atheism *á la* the cultural paradigm for the study of religion, he stresses the possibility that exists in play, which is to participate in two or more realities at the same time. Similar to how the believer takes part in a superhuman world at the same time as s/he takes part in the ordinary world in such a way that the two worlds meet and mix or at least exist on the same scale, Droogers goes for what he calls "methodological ludism" (455). He recommends that researchers leave behind their critical attitude towards religion and instead use their abilities to participate in several realities at the same time. Such an approach will be equally independent of the personal convictions of the researchers as methodological atheism or methodological agnosticism ideally should be. The "methodological ludism" will, according to Droogers, diminish the distance between the believer and the researcher. Droogers also insists that it is fruitful to analyze the metaphors of the researchers as well as the metaphors of the believers, a strategy that is, for example, followed by Johansen.

Droogers' article is one example of what could be called a postmodern approach to the study of religion with stress on relativity and reflexivity. It is furthermore an attempt to deconstruct the insider/outsider problem.

Is Droogers successful? His idea about methodological ludism is fascinating and a playful element in the study of religion should never be despised. But even if Droogers illuminates the problems of insiders and outsiders very well, he does not solve or dissolve it. In the study of a religious group, scholars of religion try to describe, understand and interpret the insider's point of view, but, all the same, scholars are not insiders. When the fieldwork is finished, the scholar will hopefully be wiser and more informed, but s/he will still remain an outsider, or go native – a point which has been stressed several times.

To speak about fields is to use metaphors. One could apply other metaphors than fields, and for instance speak about games. Are believers and scholars of religion part of the same game? They are probably best seen as part of two different games, because the non-confessional study of religion and the practice of religion follow different rules, like, for instance, chess and chequers or bridge and poker. When we, however, ask whether scholars and believers are in the same boat, the answer is affirmative, because the non-confessional study of religion is influenced by how religion is practiced and in its turn influences the practice of religion. While there are insider and outsider positions in relation to religion and the study of religion, there is no objective position that is outside everything else that exists.

Conclusion

The non-confessional study of religion has from the beginning been committed to certain norms, chief among which are the comparative approach and methodological agnosticism/neutrality. Both norms contribute to keep the non-confessional study of religion distinct from theology. Debates about norms in the study of religion are sometimes closely connected to the continuous struggle of the non-confessional study of religion to be different from theology.

Different research paradigms and various subgroups of scholars have conducted and interpreted comparison and neutrality in different ways. Rather paradoxically scholars of religion have usually been more critical towards some religions and forms of religion than towards others, and sometimes also been critical of religion *per se*. In this way opposition to religion and to forms of religion have also sometimes been among the implicit norms of a secular study of religion. The implications of such norms are not necessarily carefully thought out in the same way as the implications of the explicit norms of comparison and methodological agnosticism/neutrality are.

References

Becker, Howard S. "Whose side are we on?" *Social Problems*, 14 (1967), 239-247.
Beckford, James A. and James T. Richardson, "Religion and Regulation", in James A. Beckford and N.J. Demerath III (ed.), *The Sage Handbook of the Sociology of Religion*, Los Angeles/London: Sage Publications, 2007, 396-418.
Berger, Peter. *The Sacred Canopy*, New York: Doubleday, 1967.
Donovan, Peter. "Neutrality in Religious Studies", *Religious Studies*, 26,1 (1990), 105-115.
Droogers, André. "As Close as a Scholar Can Get. Exploring a One-Field Approach to the Study of Religion", in Hent de Vries (ed.), *Religion. Beyond a Concept*, New York: Fordham University Press, 2008, 448-463.
Frazer, James. *The Golden Bough. A Study of Comparative Religion*, London: Macmillian, 1890.
Gilhus, Ingvild Sælid. "Hva er religion i dag? Religionsbegrep og religionsvitenskap", in Arve Brunvoll, Hans Bringeland, Nils Gilje, Gunnar Skirbekk (eds.), *Religion og kultur. Ein fleirfagleg samtale*. Oslo: Universitetsforlaget, 2009, 19-31.
Hjelde, Sigurd. "Religionskritikk – noe for en religionshistoriker?" Paper Norsk religionshistorisk forening, Tromsø, 1.12.2001.

Hughes, Aaron W. "Science Envy in Theories of Religion", *Method & Theory in the Study of Religion*, 22,4 (2010), 293-303.
Jensen, Jeppe Sinding. *The study of religion in a new key: theoretical and philosophical soundings in the comparative and general study of religion*, Aarhus: Aarhus University Press, 2003.
Johansen, Birgitte Schepelern. *Adskillelsens logik. En undersøgelse af sekulære kategoriseringer af religion i akademisk praksis*. Doktorgradsavhandling Københavns universitet, Det humanistiske fakultetet, 2010.
Klimkeit, Hans-Joachim. "Friedrich Max Müller (1823-1900), in Axel Michaels (ed.), *Klassiker der Religionswissenschaft. Von Friedrich Schleiermacher bis Mircea Eliade*, München: Verlag C.H. Beck, 1997, 29-40.
Ling, Trevor *History of Religion East and West: An Introduction and Interpretation*, London: Macmillian, 1968.
Masuzawa, Tomoko. *The Invention of World Religions: Or how European universalism was preserved in the language of pluralism*, Chicago: University of Chicago Press, 2005.
McCutcheon,Russell T. *Critics not Caretakers. Redescribing the Public Study of Religion*, USA: State University of New York Press, 2001.
McCutcheon Russell T. (ed.), *The Insider/Outsider Problem in the Study of Religion. A Reader*, London and New York: Cassell, 1999.
Müller, Friedrich Max. *Chips from a German Workshop*, London: Longmans, 1867.
Müller, Friedrich Max. *Introduction to a Science of Religion*, London: Longmans, 1873.
Nye, Mallory. "Religion, post-religionism, and religioning: Religious studies and contemporary cultural debates", *Method & Theory in the Study of Religion*, 12,4, (2000), 447-476.
Sharpe, Eric J. *Comparative Religion. A History*, London: Duckworth, 1975.
Slagstad, Rune. *De nasjonale strateger*, Oslo: Pax, 1998.
Slagstad, Rune. "Styringsvitenskap – ånden som går". *Nytt Norsk Tidsskrift*, 2009, 3-4, 411-429.
Smart, Ninian. *The Science of Religion and the Sociology of Knowledge*, Princeton: Princeton University Press, 1973.
Stringer, Martin D. Contemporary Western Ethnography and the Definition of Religion, London/New York: Continuum, 2008.
Sutcliffe, Steven. "Rethinking 'New Age' as a popular religious habitus: a review essay on The Spiritual Revolution", Method & Theory in the Study of Religion, 18,3, (2006), 294-314.
Wiebe, Donald. "Does Understanding Religion Require Religious Understanding?" in Russell T. McCutcheon (ed.), *The Insider/Outsider Problem in the Study of Religion. A Reader*, London and New York: Cassell, 1999, 260-273.
Wiebe, Donald. "The Politics of Wishful Thinking? Disentangling the Role of the Scholar-Scientist from that of the Public Intellectual in the Modern Academic Study of Religion", *Temenos*, 41 (2005), 7-38.
Wiebe, Donald. "An Eternal Return All Over Again: The Religious Conversation Endures", *Journal of the American Academy of Religion*, 74, 3, (2006), 674-696.

Wissmann, Hans. "James George Frazer (1854-1941), in Axel Michaels (ed.), *Klassiker der Religionswissenschaft. Von Friedrich Schleiermacher bis Mircea Eliade*, München: Verlag C.H. Beck, 1997, 77-89.

Woodhead, Linda. "Real Religion and Fuzzy Spirituality? Taking Sides in the Sociology of Religion", in Stef Aupers & Dick Houtman (eds.), *Religions of Modernity. Relocating the Sacred to the Self and the Digital,* Leiden: Brill, 2010, 31-48.

Normativity in empirical social studies

Ole Riis

Normative challenges in the sociology of religion

Sociology of religion is generally supposed to follow 'methodological atheism' (Berger 1967 app. II). However, this does not imply that normative issues have been absent throughout its history. Sociology of religion inspired by Marx aims to reveal religion as an ideology, while church sociology aims to provide information for practical improvement of the operation of the church. A normative agenda could be traced in several empirically based studies on secularization (Brink et al 1984).

The issue of normativity can also be traced in studies of controversial new religious movements, such as Scientology. Roy Wallis' study on Scientology led him to raise critical questions about its operation (in Kristensen & Riis 1987) which led to confrontations. Bryan Wilson's report on Scientology attempted to take a neutral stance: "It is deemed essential here to avoid the value-preference implicit in such language and to employ the neutral terminology of the social sciences, whilst seeking to maintain an appropriate sensitivity to those engaged in religious activity." Wilson's report was nevertheless adopted by Scientology as appendix two of their self-presentation, right after L.Ron Hubbard's programmatic statement, *The Aims of Scientology*. Wilson's presentation has been subject to severe criticism. Thus, a critical ex-Scientologist's notices that Wilson did not see the confidential materials and failed to see "that the upper levels of Scientology are high volume dead space alien souls exorcism." (http://forums.whyweprotest.net/threads/bryan-wilson-on-scientology.–67479/.

Another example is the role of Danish researchers in the heated Danish debates about religious toleration, especially in relation to Islam. As the debates heated up in the 1980s and 1990, especially Michael Rothstein and Tim Jensen were frequently used by the media as spokesmen for religious toleration. Accordingly, they became criticized for being naïve and partisan pro-islamists. The public critique against researchers of religion were eventually widened to include researchers who regarded themselves as being neutral and balanced. The critique erupted as a team of researchers presented a report requested by the government about the prevalence of burka and niqab in Denmark (Rapport 2009). The report gave a relatively low estimate of the number of women wearing burqa and niqab, based on information from spokespersons for Muslim communities and various researchers. Immediately after its publication, the report became subject to severe criticism. The influential spokesman for the Conservatives on immigration issues, Naser Khader, commented that he could not understand how university employees could make such a painful report. (Kristeligt Dagblad 19.1. 2010.). The leader of the populist Dansk Folkeparti, Pia Kjærsgaard, criticized the report for having obtained information from 'extremists', and she suggested to subject the report to the national committee against scientific fraud (Universitetsavisen 19.1. 2010). This represents an open attempt to influence the direction of religion through political power.

At the turn of the new millennium, religion has re-emerged as an issue in social discourses. Sociology of religion therefore provides information which can be used and misused by the parties in order to support their opinions, values, and interests. If sociologists of religion withdraw from the debates, they become redundant; and if they engage in the debates, they can be accused of partisanship. Sociologists of religion are thus involved in the issue of religious confrontations and in the discourse on religious toleration, whether they want to or not. The issue of religious pluralism and discrimination is one where the challenge of values is hard to avoid. The researcher therefore has to consider how the arguments can be interpreted and how the empirical findings can be used by the parties in the discourse.

These examples illustrate that sociology of religion has been involved in several normative discourses, willingly or unwillingly. The critique of Positivism also raised the question whether a 'value-free' position is possible and tenable. Questions about normativity emerge whenever science takes up issues which are subject to a polarized discourse in society. Social research is situated on this earth, in a historical situation where society may be divided and where information is used as a weapon in discourse. Research can only be 'objective' by ignoring the issues of the conflict, and then it will not be relevant to society. When researchers become subject to public critique, some take an empiricist stand and produce facts, and some refer to established norms for research ethics, such as Robert K. Merton's (cf. below). Some may take an explicit normative stand. This is hardly noticed when their norms correspond with the predominant values and are rendered in a 'politically correct' language. Some dare propose contested norms. Social research has a long tradition of value-oriented research. One of the major schools is that of Critical Social Research, which we will discuss in the following. One of its major thinkers, Jürgen

Habermas, is also a chief figure in debates on democracy and religious toleration.

Attempts at value-free social research

'Normativity' is often used as a term which criticizes research for being dictated by values. Thus, research can be criticized for being prejudiced, biased, or ideological. Such a critique is reasonable if the research is dictated by implicit values. It is thus reasonable to criticize research for being carried by prejudice or ideology, performed in a biased manner by selecting only cases which affirm the value-based prejudgment. However, it is problematic when this critique goes on to demand that research becomes objective, neutral and completely balanced. It is questionable both whether this is possible in practice and whether human and social relevance does not imply a value-orientation. The critique against normativity mixes whether research is value-dictated or value-oriented, and whether the values are explicit or implicit.

Efforts to purify research of normativity is based on the presupposition that we can draw a clear line of demarcation between descriptive and normative statements, between 'is' and 'ought'. This distinction is derived from Hume's *Treatise of Human Nature* (1739-40), where he argued that we cannot draw a normative conclusion from descriptive premises. For example, when we consider the facts about a murder, we cannot find any fact which can be depicted as inherently evil. Our judgment is emotional, not related to the action as such. Hume's distinction between facts and values is discussed in other articles in this anthology. His argument influenced Positivism. Hempel, for instance, argued that: "The grounds on which scientific hypotheses are accepted or rejected are provided by empirical evidence, which may influence observational findings as well as previous established laws and theories, but surely no value judgments." (1965, 91)

Hume's distinction between facts and values divided intellectual efforts into a search for objective, factual knowledge on the one hand and subjective evaluations on the other. However, empiricism only seems 'objective' on the surface. Descriptive research typically avoids presenting the epistemological and ontological premises. It collects 'data', which are assumed to be given by nature; not selected and produced by human researchers. Empirical induction conflates reality with what is directly observable. This represents an epistemic fallacy. An empirical description is rendered in a theoretical language, which has implicit values. A theoretical perspective thus opens for analysing some value issues while it excludes others. Empiricist science has lost its Positivistic legitimacy, but it continues as a paradigm in many branches of research.

Max Weber's discussion on 'objectivity and 'value judgments' in social research superficially seems to correspond with that of Positivism. However, as a neo-Kantian, Weber noticed that our recognition of even the most grounded theoretical statements remains a cultural product. The kind of social research presented by the journal *Archiv* aims to address political and social problems, and such problems cannot be solved by technical considerations referring to a given goal; the measure standards for regulations can and must be contended. Therefore, Weber's notion of 'value-freedom' does not depend on producing 'objective facts', as in Positivism. Weber emphatically argued that discussions about values are not meaningless for social research. The social sciences need to address practical problems and trace unreflected value judgments back to their originating ideas. However, it is not the task of any empirical science to formulate a practical common denominator for our problems in the form of generally valid, fundamental ideals. According to Weber (2003/1904) values can be permitted as research subjects, and in the contextual definition of the research problem, but the analysis must lead to the same conclusion, independent of the analysts' values (Weber 1904). It may be said that Weber proposes scientific 'value-freedom' as a necessary precondition for a scientific value-analysis and critique of value-judgments. This indicates that Weber's notion of 'value-freedom' is more complex than a demand for 'neutrality. 'Objectivity' is consistently bracketed by Weber, and his arguments are methodological rather than epistemological. Furthermore, his later (1913) memorandum on 'value-freedom' should be read on the background of the contemporary debate about political commentaries ex cathedra by university professors.

In present social research, Robert K. Merton's norms are widely accepted. He stressed that 'They are moral as well as technical prescriptions.' They were formulated on the background of state-directed and state-censored research in the 20th century. His four imperatives include: 1. "Universalism", truth claims are subjected to pre-established impersonal criteria, 2. "Communism", the substantive findings of science are a product of social collaboration and are assigned to the community. 3. "Disinterestedness", a distinctive pattern of institutional control of a wide range of motives which characterizes the behavior of scientists. 4. "Organized skepticism", the suspension of judgment until 'the facts are at hand' and the detached scrutiny of beliefs in terms of empirical and logical criteria. This set of scientific imperatives is derived from reflections on the role of science in a democratic society. Merton notes that many scientific statements are incomprehensible to the general public, while democratic decisions depend on scientific evidence. Therefore, a system of collective control is necessary for science, the ultimate accountability of scientists to their com-peers.

Merton's imperatives are based on moral and political arguments. These criteria are in themselves normative. They point to a moral obligation for scientific institutions and a moral responsibility for individual researchers. Merton notices that 'organized scepticism' involves a latent source of critique: "a latent questioning of certain bases of established routine, authority, vested procedures and the real of the 'sacred' generally" (p. 547) One criterion is especially pertinent in a discussion on normativity in empirical studies, namely 'disinterestedness'. This could be read as an effort to elevate science to a perspective of distanced, uninvolved observers. However, that is hardly what Merton aims at. Disinterestedness does not refer to the singular scientist but to the control of the institution, where 'cultism, informal cliques, prolific but trivial institutions' become subject to qualified critique. However, Merton's arguments are influenced by Positivism which was predominant when he wrote references to 'facts', and 'empirical and logical evidence', but he does not consider 'interpretations'.

These arguments from Positivists and Weberians still form the foundation of 'value relativism' in social research, based on a distinction between descriptive and normative judgments, and on implicit norms for research and rational discourse. Value relativism argues that value judgements can only be warranted by references to other value judgments, while descriptive judgments can be warranted by direct empirical reference. Thus, value judgments cannot be warranted empirically and rationally.

Critique of value-relativism

Many philosophers and researchers have argued against value relativism from Hume to modern value relativism from many perspectives. The main problem is that value relativism – in its empiricist version - presupposes that humans can obtain a direct access to the given, empirical world, and research aims at describing this objectively. It is dubious whether any descriptive claims can be regarded as 'self-warranted'.

The Canadian philosopher, Charles Taylor, is a contemporary critic of value relativism. He demonstrates that political theories which are regarded as purely empirical have clear and plausible normative implications (1995). Thus, the basic distinction between descriptive and normative statements is problematic. The demarcation line between descriptive and normative statements is necessarily blurred. Whether a statement is descriptive or normative depends on its context, not on its content alone. The statement "Its too hot to work" seems purely evaluative, but it means the same as "The thermometer shows 17 degrees Celsius, so the ice sculpture can hardly be made now", which is a factual statement.

If we pursue his arguments, scientific reasoning can hardly be based only on purely descriptive statements, cleansed from any evaluative implications. Furthermore, a rational reasoning does not preclude evaluative arguments. If that were the case, all legal verdicts would become irrational. The rationality of scientific reasoning does not depend on excluding all evaluations but rather on making them explicit and on providing convincing arguments for them. This approach to values differs basically from Weber who regarded the discourse on values as a battlefield of contradictions and oppositions. This rationalistic perspective seems too narrow. The discourse on values can be pursued with mutual toleration and understanding, as a 'rational' discourse where the participants investigate whether their values are identical, supplementary, compatible, or contradictory and even in conflict. Such discourses are not derived from empirical facts, but the arguments will of course refer to such facts.

However, research can also be normative in a positive sense. This is the case with applied research, which sets up certain goals and investigates how they can be realized. A further variety is mobilizing research which aims to help a certain group to realize their shared interests. This was, for instance, the case with the Neo-Marxist approach of the 1960s. In a much larger perspective, Critical Social Research seeks to emancipate human agents from unnecessary, unwarranted, or illegitimate limitations of their life possibilities. From this point of view, normativity is positive and even necessary for the development of a more human society.

In a positive sense, 'normativity' implies warranting research claims based on value judgements by reference to a set of explicit norms. Thereby, the value judgements are not arbitrary or subjective but can be subject to a rational, inter-subjective discourse. A claim about a social situation can be warranted by a rational scheme of argumentation which includes both descriptive and evaluative components. While the description is grounded in shared experiences, the evaluation refers to shared norms. Arguments which combine facts and values are well-known in law courts, politics management, and in everyday social life. By propagating a stance of value-freedom – as Parsons (1965), Lazarsfeld, and Rossi – sociology is restricted to provide empirical facts which other parties may use for their value-oriented decisions. Abstracted empirical social research thus follows a 'bureaucratic ethos' according to C.W. Mills (1970 114). Social research is thereby excluded from criticizing the usage of its findings. Mills argued that anyone who spends his life studying society and publishing the results is acting morally and usually politically as well.

The issue of normativity posits research as a societal institution. Research is financed by outside sources, by the state, by corporations, by funds, and organizations, and it is held responsible by its sources. Some very privileged academics assume that they only have an internal responsibility, to their own colleagues. That is an illusion. The discussion about normativity relates to whom research is responsible in society. In the final instance, research is financed because it is expected to produce information which has potentials for practical use. So the big question is, who can use social research and for which aims?

The quest for objectivity

The critique of 'normativity' in research often refers to an ideal of 'objectivity'. However, as noticed by Andrew Sayer (2000), 'objectivity/subjectivity' has three independent meanings: 1) it can refer to a value-free perspective, versus a value-laden one; 2) it can refer to epistemology: true or practically adequate knowledge versus personal opinion; 3) it can refer to ontology, to objective properties of the nature of things, regardless of what we may think about them versus properties pertaining to subjects, or the situated and embodied character of knowledge. The third meaning of objectivity concerns the 'intransitive' dimension of science. Whereas our experiences and ideas about the world change – transitively – the world as such does not change. In other words, the world should not be conflated with our experience of it. The former two meanings of objectivity are often conflated and confused, so it is assumed that in order to arrive at true statements those statements must be value-neutral. This conflation is based on efforts to draw a distinction between facts and values, and the emotivist assumption that values are beyond reason, incapable of having any objective content. Both positivists and relativists make this conflation. For positivists, science must be value-free in order to provide truth, for relativists, science only produces various narratives and it is impossible to assess their truth.

Intransitive 'facts' refer to realities which are assumed to exist independently of our interpretation. We can and will encounter negative consequences if we ignore or misunderstand the factual conditions. While we may draw a clear distinction between a physical object and our description of it, it is more problematic when the object is a social construct. Social institutions, such as money or laws, can be regarded as 'real constructs', since they have a real impact on social life, despite their being socially constructed. Also, religion can function as a 'real construct', for instance when heretics or witches were condemned to the bonfire. While we cannot change natural laws, like the law of gravity, socially constructed laws and norms can be modified or annulled. Thus, approaches to social constructions call for a dual stance which recognizes both its transitive and intransitive dimensions. Otherwise, economic fluctuations may be described ideologically as dictated by natural laws, or social stratification as directed by divine providence.

Knowledge is formed by social language, which is not a transparent, stable, consistent medium. Nevertheless, we can produce knowledge of the world which we must rationally agree on as reliable. We may not be able to provide objective proofs, and all the evidence provided is based on human observations and communicated by human language. Still, we can establish rational rules for a discourse and evaluation of the fallible claims about the world which we discuss. Whereas the world must be regarded as an entity, our human minds cannot grasp this in a holistic manner. We have to identify the dimensions by which we structure our interpretation and clarify their relevance for focusing on and distinguishing between human experiences. This selection is, however, necessarily subject to discussion and modification.

Whereas value judgments cannot be warranted in an objective sense, they can still be warranted in an inter-subjective sense, a point discussed by Henriksen in this volume. This is exactly what judges must do in a murder verdict when they weigh the empirical evidence, judgments about value motives of the accused, and value judgments about the social consequences of the act. Descriptive 'facts' are valued according to their relevance to the judgment of the act, and evaluative judgments are valued according to whether they are supported by 'facts'. Despite being value-related, the judgement is far from subjective and arbitrary. Other judges will probably draw the same conclusion, based on the facts and the legal system.

Despite the wide-spread claim that it is impossible to discuss subjective taste rationally, this is actually done when critics evaluate films, music, or technical equipment. For instance, magazines which evaluate hi-fi-equipment only refer to the objective data as background information, while the main judgment depends on a value-related subjective auditing. In order to make the evaluation credible for the readers, the reviewer has to explicate the values and how they were applied.

Any description of human perception of the world has to be formed by a human language which is value-related. Humans construct a linguistic interpretation of their notions about what 'is', which has implicit associations with 'oughts'. Scientific descriptions of the world are also social constructions, which leads to a challenge of the distinction between facts and valuations. The criticism of objectivism has led constructivists to take the counter-position of value relativism, which accepts a value-perspective, albeit only as personal opinions. Humans, including human researchers, perceive and interpret the world in different manners. Radical constructivism regards theories as 'narratives', or tales based on a perspective directed by arbitrary, subjective values. Such an individualistic value perspective does not open for a discourse about how we as thinking, perceiving and acting human beings can relate to the world we share our lives in. Even if we do not have 'objective' depictions of 'the real world', the descriptions are rendered in a shared language, embedded in a shared world and refer to aspects of an interdependent social life. Our evaluation of the credibility of a depiction influences how we live together, and embeds our individual biographies in a shared history. However, the position of value-relativism does not allow for a discourse about the credibility and consequences of various narratives. While it embraces normativity, it does not open for a discussion and a social evaluation of the implied values.

Critical theory

From its origin, sociology was seen as a branch of science which could provide information for reforming and improving society. Saint-Simon's vision of a Positivistic social research was related to social values. It is even possible to trace value-relations through the study on life of the unemployed in Marienthal, performed by researchers affiliated with the Positivistic Vienna School (Jahoda et al). Social studies based on Marxism were value-related and often even value-directed. However, value-relations can also be traced in other branches of social research. In the USA, the Chicago school took up social problems in the town seen from the perspective of 'the underdog'. In the UK, Fabian social researchers initiated a programme which aimed at discovering how "economic equity can be arrived at through democratic decision-making (1998, 289)" by "rigorous empirical investigation" (1998, 286), in the words of Beatrice Webb. These schools represented the view that social research should not just produce descriptions of routine behavior and affirm common assumptions about society but provide information which challenged them and could help improve social conditions.

The issue of a value-related critical reflection has been especially explicit in the Critical Theory of the Frankfurt School. It aims to unveil biases and ideologies, questions taken-for-granted views, and points to their negative consequences. Critical research can be based on a rational or practical critique, which is based on certain values. A normative critique involves an explicit argument for the premises. Theory is regarded as a contribution to recognize the basic character of (capitalist) society and realize a 'true society' which is reasonable and just, and thus normative in both a scientific and political sense. (Sørensen in Jacobsen 2010)

The Frankfurt school was established in Germany in the traumatic era after the First World War, which demonstrated the destructive capacity of modern technology. Germany in the mid-war era was subject to economic and political crises and clashes in the streets between Fascists and Communists. Anti-semitism was evoked as part of the Nazi agenda for a national revival. It was also an era where modern tools of mass manipulation emerged. In a crisis-prone society where ideologies predominated, the Frankfurt school tried to maintain a rational research agenda, based on humanitarian, socialist values. The critique is inspired by Marx, but it also expressed disillusion with Marxism as a political programme. Most of its members had to flee, mainly to the USA. In their refuge, they experienced a limiting kind of freedom which became a focus of their later criticism.

The approach of Critical Social Theory can be characterized as a combination of Marxist economic functionalism and a Weberian view on purposive rationality as a major feature of the modern mind. Modern society is thus regarded as a monolithic culture, organized by a collaboration of state and capitalism, in an interlocked combination of administrative social control and individual willingness to conform. This view of the monolithic social system has pervaded much social critique since its origin during the Nazi rule and the Second World War. For instance, its critique still resonates in critique of commercialized mass culture. This perspective on society corresponded fairly well to tendencies in the era of industrialization: a productive system which demanded discipline and self-discipline of work, and an expansion of standardized material values. It corresponds less well with tendencies in societies where the industrial sector is receding while the service sector is expanding (Bell 1973), and where material values (material and political security) are superseded by 'post-material' values (social, aesthetical and self-realization values) (Inglehart 1990).

Both Capitalist and Communist societies follow a Baconian ideal of technological progress. This became subject to criticism by Adorno (1972) and Horkheimer, who regarded it as human domination over natural objects through a narrow instrumental rationality, characterized by objectivized thoughts, reification of nature and disciplined labour. This was concomitant with the human mastery of nature and the mastery of human nature by Fascist rule. Societal labour is in itself a source of alienation, while emancipation is human reconciliation with nature.

The heritage of the Frankfurt school: Habermas

The social critique of the Frankfurt school can be read as a desperate appeal to reason. It hardly had much impact on social discourse beyond the intellectual elite which shared its premises. This is contrasted by the status of its successor, Jürgen Habermas. He is both influenced by and critical of the Frankfurt school. He pursues its agenda of a critical discourse of society. However, he has not accepted the functionalistic and narrowly rationalistic premises of its critique. His discussion of society includes a constellation of the political and economic social system regulated by the media of power and money on the one hand and the life world of human interaction on the other. While the former Frankfurt school's critique was based on an instrumental rationality, Habermas expanded this by adding a communicative rationality. Thereby, Habermas' critique escaped from being caught in fatalism. Communicative rationality points to a critique and a residue of opposition. The opposition between demands from the system and human considerations of the life world forms the major pathology of modernity: "The rationalization of the lifeworld makes possible an increase in system complexity which enlarges to such an extent that the released system outstrips the comprehension ability of the lifeworld which is instrumentalized by them" (Habermas 1981 p. 232 ff.)

Habermas' criticism is based on explicating the values of a democratic society. It is from this value-perspective that he is able to criticize certain tendencies in existing society. Habermas' model of democracy has been subject to discussion. Honneth has also criticized his yielding to the 'seductions of systems theory', which may lead to a surrender of the critical potential of his communicative-theoretical approach. (1987). By proposing a dualist approach, Habermas opens up for a compromise between a systems-affirmative view and a communicative-critical one. However, he does not indicate when influence from the system on the lifeworld becomes dysfunctional for society at large. We may add that the functional arguments of Habermas are based on a set of explicit, debatable values, whereas the former functionalism of Talcott Parsons was based on implicit values.

Jürgen Habermas' famous discussion of knowledge and human interest originates from 1965. It was then a shattering dual critique against on the one hand Positivism and on the other abstract hermeneutics. The first part of this critique has become clichées among advocates for the humanities, while the second part is often ignored by them. It is therefore worth reconsidering his arguments. According to Habermas,

> ...the positivistic self-understanding of the nomological sciences lends countenance to the substitution of technology for enlightened action. It directs the utilization of scientific information from an illusory viewpoint, namely that the practical matter of history can be reduced to technical control of objectified processes. The objectivist self-understanding of the hermeneutic sciences is of no lesser consequence. It defends sterilized knowledge and locks up history in a museum. Guided by the objectivistic attitude of theory as the image of facts, the nomological and hermeneutical sciences reinforce each other with regard to their practical consequences (1972, 317).

Habermas argues that the viewpoints from which we apprehend reality ground three categories of possible knowledge: information that expands our power of technical control and is applied in work as a productive force; interpretations that enable social action within common traditions, communicated by language; and critical analyses of legitimations that free consciousness from its dependence on hypostasized powers (1972, 308-17). Corresponding with this, Apel formulates three fundamental interests of knowledge: The interest in controlling an objectified environmental world; the interest in communicative understanding; and the interest in critically emancipatory self-reflection (1977 425-28). Apel stresses that the second interest refers to both the understanding of meaning and the coming to agreement. He refers to it as *Verständigungs-Interesse*, interest in an intersubjective comprehension. Apel claims that these three fundamental interests of knowledge are presupposed in all types of scientific enquiries but certain types of science are paradigmatically determined by one of these. They supplement and exclude each other and cannot be reduced to each other.

By recognizing a connection between knowledge and interests a question emerges concerning whether all humans share their interests. Habermas seems to assume that all rational humans can reach a consensus about their common interests in living together in a democratic society. When science is not allowed to demand acceptance of its view as objective truth and absolute rationality, it can only appeal to human reason and mutual consideration. This approach follows from the Enlightenment and the struggle for a liberal democracy. It is based on a historically determined view on human knowledge and social life. It is based on a view of humans as autonomous entities which should be convinced by rational arguments about their personal and common interests. It does not naively presume that the conditions for consensus and consent are present, but it tries to support these conditions by forwarding reasons for an open, rational discourse. Habermas has stressed language as a basic tool developing agreement about knowledge interests. He argues that the universal human interest in autonomy and responsibility can be apprehended a priori through the structure of language.

As noted above, a general sceptical criticism from an individual perspective contributes to a centrifugal force in society, which disperses the critique and weakens its impact. This stance is averted by recent critical Theory by arguing for emancipation of humankind rather than individual freedom, and for producing problem-solving knowledge rather than narratives.

A critique of Critical Theory

Social science is part of a discourse in society. It can provide information about how to manipulate and suppress people or how to empower and emancipate them. It can provide information which may support the status quo or challenge it and change social structure. Therefore, social research has an ethical obligation to reflect upon the potential application of its findings beyond the academic community. Research is the institutionalized production of valid knowledge in modern society. Proposals for decisions in society are legitimated by referring to asserted knowledge. As resources for research are limited, different branches and projects have to be prioritized. This involves value judgments. Those who fund research may, of course, appeal to values, which are claimed to be universal. However, evaluation of which types of knowledge are especially needed depend on socially embedded values. In a differentiated society, there are divergent views on which types of knowledge are needed and which projects should be funded. Those values which predominate in the leading – economic and political - sectors of society will also have an influence on priorities of research. Even the universities, which give their researchers autonomy regarding their choice of problem, are obliged by major institutions in society to produce knowledge, which is regarded as relevant and preferably also applicable by them.

Society is differentiated, and accordingly, social relations can be studied from many different perspectives. In a differentiated society, there are divergent interests regarding which types of research problems are especially relevant, and which research perspectives ought to be presented. This challenge has led to considerations about 'situated knowledge'. One classic example of situated knowledge is the Marxist notion that the view of the economically dominant class prevails as a social perspective. According to Marxism, social interests are fundamentally based on antagonistic class perspectives. If members of the suppressed class were to take the perspective of the dominant class, their thoughts would be "false consciousness." Also critical feminist theory, where gender determined the cognitive perspective, exemplifies situated knowledge. In a similar manner, Pierre Bourdieu argues that science is a social field like others, where particular parties compete in order to obtain the involved capitals. A further example is Michel Foucault who regards science as a power-directed discourse of power in a society among others, where people interpret the world and their life. Such arguments for situated knowledge are based on particularistic value perspectives. However, situated knowledge typically presents one perspective as right, namely that of the postulated suppressed group. It typically omits considering its relation to other perspectives. Social perspectives are supposed to be mutually exclusive and even antagonistic. However, this represents an extreme structural constellation.

Situated perspectives form a range of structural constellations, which include opposition, contradiction, competition, complementarity, and convergence. In many differentiated social situations, the perspectives are neither identical nor conflicting but complementary. Actors and spectators have different perspectives on a performance, politicians and voters have different perspectives on an election, musicians and the audience have different perspectives on a concert. But in most cases, these perspectives complement each other and form a functioning situation for both parties. Each party of the encounter wish to have their opposite party understand their perspective, but also that they cannot and should not adopt it entirely.

Critical sociology typically takes into perspective those who are assumed to be suppressed by those who predominate in society and who directly or indirectly influence discourse in society. For instance, critical ethnographies aim to produce a better understanding of marginal groups by presenting their own perspective of social life. Such studies have a legitimate value perspective, namely to profile the invisible, talk for the mute, and assist the powerless. There is, however, an implicit risk in presenting only one perspective on social life. Biographies of life at the margin of society contain a risk of becoming entertainment for the cultural elite rather than a means of emancipation. Bourdieu's seminal description of the misery of social conditions (1993) is critical in a basic sense, as it allows the reader to sympathize with the presented victims. Their biographies provide a better understanding of how the victims experience their situation. However, this does not indicate their relations to each other or structural pressures or indicate any way out of misery. Critical ethnographies are contrasted by structuralist criticism, which points to suppressing and dehumanizing consequences of the macro-social system, without investigating how the structures are experienced and handled. Structuralist criticism thus seems to assume that people will rise spontaneously in protest or revolution as the power structure is revealed to them. The right criterion for evaluating critical research is whether it actually aids the people it talks for, and this is questionable in some cases. It is noticeable how seldom critical social research is required, financed and applauded by the people it is supposed to assist.

Critical ethnographies open for understanding the values of a set of people which may deviate from the predominant values in society. Critical ethnographies thus present values. It also opens for 'reflexivity', or a self-critique of the researcher's value-perspective. Reflexivity was coined as a term by Gouldner and adopted by Bourdieu as a key to his social critique.

However, this line of critical ethnography refrains from engaging in a discussion of values. A presentation and analytical understanding of these values does not necessarily imply acceptance of them. By understanding the values of a psychopathic informant, we may realize how dangerous that person is. While this approach opens for explicating the values presented by the research and the values of the involved researcher, it does not open up for a general discussion on values. This restricts its potential for inspiring changes in social practices and social structures.

The basic approach to social agents has consequences for the applicability of the study. An individualistic, hermeneutical approach has the advantage that readers can understand agents with other horizons. But a purely individualistic approach limits the potentials for changing the conditions. Individual actors can hardly change the structures by spontaneous protests. To change structures and institutions calls for a co-ordinated mobilization. Sociological research can make people aware of the structural conditions of problems which are seen as personal, and thereby inspire a potential for change by mobilizing protest or by influencing policies.

The aim of emancipation presupposes research on manifest and emergent causality inn society. Causality should not be understood in the behavioristic sense of observing empirical regularities. Discourses can produce changes and be causes in a wider sense. An investigation of emancipation implies a distinction between necessity and possibility. In order to consider alternatives, it is necessary to begin with studying the restraints of status quo. Otherwise, the study would only produce a utopian vision. Some of the stabilizing mechanisms can hardly be omitted or changed, but some can be blocked or modified. A study which is aimed at social emancipation should indicate which causal mechanisms could become operative for social transformation.

A critique of ideologies make the human agents aware that conditions which they have considered necessary – where 'is' becomes 'ought' - are in fact changeable. A critique of ideology reveals that conditions which are reluctantly accepted as necessary are in fact changeable products of their own actions. So far, this critique of ideology corresponds with Anthony Giddens. However, his approach is carried by double hermeneutics, which regards ideology as a misrepresentation of social constructions as necessary, while it does not consider ideology as unrecognized structural determination of social life.

A critique of values takes a different stance, as it refers to objective conditions but discusses their evaluation. It assumes that the conditions can be studied as real, as objective realities or as real social constructs. The issue is the criteria of evaluation. Focus is on which values agents living under the specified conditions ought to pursue. This further leads to a discussion of why the agents accept values of the hegemony and why they conform and adapt to society. A critique of values is often implied in studies of real conditions. For instance, the usage of alcohol and drugs by young persons may lead to confront issues about values and life-styles and indicate policies for value-change. An 'objective' description may reveal problems, which are 'inherent' in the sense that there are no rational arguments for maintaining the status quo.

Critical research can point to unintended consequences of social actions, it can reveal hidden structures of power and latent potentials for changes, it can indicate alternatives to the social structure, and point to conditions for mobilizing social change. Social descriptions try to describe how the situation is, while critical theory asks whether it is necessary and acceptable. Hermeneutical studies provide indications of how people understand their situations, but critical theory raises questions about whether their understanding has been manipulated towards a particular perspective which poses the 'is' of status quo as an 'ought'. Ordinary explanatory studies point to law-like patterns of behaviour, while critical theory asks about emergent mechanisms which could change behavioural patterns. Functional studies focus on how society can operate as an effective entity and how structures can be reproduced and stabilized, while critical research challenges the notion of an entity based on a shared value foundation, and seeks possible alternatives to the existing type of society.

Critical, reflexive praxis

Social critique implies a contribution to an evaluative discourse in society. It does not merely mean to point out problems or negative features. Social critique contributes to evaluative reflections on social and cultural life. It is based on empirical studies, but goes beyond them by addressing evaluative questions about their relevance, applicability and potential for contributions to improve social life and in a larger perspective to emancipate humanity. This leads us to address the issue of the application of social research. "Die Philosophen haben die Welt nur vershieden *interpretiert,* es kömmt drauf an, sie zu *verändern"* says Karl Marx in the 11 thesis on Feuerbach (1845). This is the basic point of critical theory, although we do not need to follow Marx' values.

Critical knowledge is not just a reflection of social conditions, an active, practice-oriented knowledge. Our knowledge about the world and our understanding of social life enables us to improve human conditions. This does not imply a utilitarian stance where the world is regarded as raw material and other people as instruments or obstacles. It implies ethical reflections about our values and our involvement in the world and in society. A practice-directed, critical research combines empirical studies of actual social life with phenomenological and hermeneutical research on the experience and interpretation of it, and further projects on actual alternatives to social life. This research also involves ethical reflections about the intentions of the researchers, on the consequences of the findings, and on their correspondence with ethical maxims and basic values. The issue of normativity basically addresses the relation between research ethics and social ethics. It confronts research with a social responsibility and asks for what and for who the knowledge is produced. An answer calls for reflections on the implicit or explicit value-relation of research.

A self-critical reflectivity involves arguing explicitly for the choice of values in research. In some cases, research is related to particularistic values, such as class, a gender, or stakeholders, in some cases, research is related to values which are held as universal, such as human emancipation, democracy, affluence or social order. In either case, the researcher is obliged to argue for the legitimacy of the values. For instance, emancipation has many meanings, so it is necessary to clarify who are to be freed, from what and to what.

An ethical reflexion also involves considerations about research designs and methods. According to research design, humans are regarded as reactants, respondents, informants, objects, deciders, participants and so forth. Research designs do not only point to strategies for collecting and analyzing information. They also indicate ethical responsibilities to the involved persons and to society at large.

A critical praxis combines empirical, ethical and practical aspects of research. Empiricism omits addressing the ethical challenges of research. Ethical discourse omits addressing empirical studies which could illustrate the conditions of people's responsibility. Utilitarian research is oriented towards a narrow set of goals and it considers means for obtaining it, without considering the wider consequences of the initiatives. By combining empirical, practical and ethical aspects, critical research is also engaged in more complex reflexion.

A critical social research can utilize the methodological toolbox of empirical research in order to describe the initial conditions and understand the perspectives of the agents. However, in order to illuminate the probable future and possible alternatives, it needs to add less common research designs, such as forecasting, scenarios, projections, and simulations. Such designs are well-established and widely used by other disciplines, such as economists, political scientists and ecologists. In order to open up for an evaluative discussion of how to form, present and discuss these alternatives, an ethical framework has to be added. This also involves discussing the value relevance of research, the dissemination of research, and the application of it. One issue is whether a study makes the agents involved realize their situation and possibilities for improving it. An emancipator study aims to empower human agents with active knowledge about their real options. This kind of critical social research involves ethics as a guidance for identifying social problems and producing and disseminating knowledge which can answer the problems in practice. A hermeneutical aspect is involved since it involves making human agents realize their situation, and their possibilities for changing it. It involves giving the agents involved options and thereby a responsibility. The knowledge aims to make the agents realize that the problems are not natural, necessary or determined by destiny. A confrontation with such ideas involves a critique of ideology. Furthermore, in order to be able to change their situation, the agents have to know what is objectively given, which mechanisms of change are available, and what is needed for changing the situation. Critical social research thus aims to disseminate a practice-oriented knowledge among the involved agents about their personal situation and their collective potentials for changing it.

The evaluation of critical social research depends on practice: whether it empowers agents to clarify their values and initiate a cooperative action in order to improve their shared situation. The programme of critical social research is practice-oriented and thereby resembles pragmatism or even the social technology criticized by Critical Theory. What demarcates this type of critical praxis from social technology is its ethical stance and explicit discourse on values, where social technology regards humans as reactants to stimuli from active manipulators, critical praxis respects humans as reflecting agents who are called to participate with an active responsibility in the process of transformation. This responsibility is not limited to those agents who are directly involved in the process, but includes those who are directly and indirectly influenced by it, including their successors.

References

Adorno, Theodor. *Soziologische Schriften*. Frankfurt a. M.: EA., 1972, 1975.
Apel,, Karl-Otto. "Types of Social Research in the Light of Human Interests of Knowledge." *Social research* 44 (3), 1977, 425-470.
Bacon, Francis. *Novum Organon*, 1620, commented by Thomas Fowler, Bibliolife on books.google.com)
Bell, Daniel. *The Coming of Post-Industrial Society*. New York: Basic Books. 1973.
Bourdieu, Pierre. *La Misère du monde*. Paris: Seuil, 1993.
Bulmer, Martin. *The Chicago School of Sociology: Institutionalization, Diversity, and the Rise of Sociological Research*. Chicago: University of Chicago Press, 1984.
Delanty, Gerard & Strydom, Piet (Eds). *Philosophies of the Social Sciences*. Maidenhead, Philadelphia: Open University Press, 2003.
Giddens, Anthony & Turner, B. (Eds). *Social Theory Today*. Stanford: Stanford University Press, 1987.
Giddens, Anthony. *Central Problems in Social Theory*. London: Macmillan, 1979.
Habermas, Jürgen. "Erkenntnis und Interesse". In: *Technologie und Wissenschaft als 'Ideologie'*. Frankfurt a. M.: Suhrkamp, 1969.
Habermas, Jürgen. *Knowledge and Human Interests*. London: Heinemann, 1972.
Habermas, Jürgen. *Theorie des kommunikativen Handelns*. Frankfurt a.M.: Suhrkamp, 1981.
Horkheimer, Max & Adorno, Theodor W. *Dialektik der Aufklärung*. In: Adorno: *Gesammelte Schriften 3*. Frankfurt a. M.: Suhrkamp, 1981.
Hempel, C. G. *Aspects of Scientific Explanation and Other Essays in the Philosophy of Science*. New York: Free Press, 1965.
Hume, David. *A Treatise on Human Nature*. Oxford. Oxford University Press, 2007 (originally published 1739-40).
Inglehart, Ronald. *Culture Shift in Advanced Industrial Society*. Princeton. Princeton University Press, 1990.
Jacobsen, Michael Hviid et al (red). *Videnskabsteori*. København: Hans Reitzels Forlag, 2010.
Jahoha, Maria et al. *Marienthal. The Sociolography of an Unemployed Community*. New Brunswick: Transaction Publishers, 2002.
Kristensen, Ragnhild & Ole Riis (red.). *Religiøse minoriteter*. Århus: Aarhus Universitetsforlag, 1987.
Lengermann, P. M., & Niebrugge-Brantley, J. *The women founders: Sociology and social theory 1830-1930*. New York: McGraw-Hill Companies, 1998.
Marx, Karl. *Marx-Engels Gesamtausgabe* I/5. Pp 533-5. Moscow, 1945.

Merton, Robert K. *Social Theory and Social Structure*. Glencoe, Illinois: The Free Press, 1957.
Mills, C. W. *The Sociological Imagination*. Harmondsworth: Penguin 1970.
Rapport om brug af niqab og burka. Institut for tværkulturelle og regionale studier. Københavns Universitet 2009. Accessed on: http://www.e-pages.dk/ku/322/
Parsons, Talcott, "Evaluation and objectivity in social science: an interpretation of Max Weber's contribution". *International Journal of the Social sciences* (15), 1965, 196-204.
Sayer, Andrew: *Realism and Social Science*. London: Sage, 2000.
Skjervheim, Hans: *Deltaker og tilskoder og andre essays*. Oslo: Tanum-Norli, 1976.
Taylor, Charles. "Neutrality in Political Science". In: *Philosophy and the Human Sciences – Philosophical Papers 2*. Cambridge: Cambridge University Press, 1995.
Weber, Max. „Die 'Objektivität' sozialwissenschaftlicher und sozialpolitischer Erkenntnis." Pp 146-214 in: *Gesammelte Aufsätze zur Wissenschaftslehre*. Tübingen: J.C.B. Mohr Verlag, 1998 (Org. 1904).
Wilson, Bryan, Website reference accessed 13.1.2011.
http://www.bonafidescientology.org/Append/02/page09.htm

Cultural empirical studies and normativity:
A case from missiology

Kari Storstein Haug

Introduction

In this article I will address some of the methodological challenges related to using empirical material in a missiological research project. The main question is: What kind of problems arise when combining empirical material and normative theological discussion, and how can they be approached? My own PhD thesis titled *"As you sow, you will reap": Interpreting Proverbs 11:18-31, Psalm 73, and Ecclesiastes 9:1-12 in Light of, and as a Response to Thai Buddhist Interpretations. A Contribution to Christian-Buddhist Dialogue*[1] will be used as a case. Based on this case, I will present and discuss some of the issues and problems I considered with regard to the relationship between empirical research and normativity, and also critically reflect on some of the deficiencies in the project with regard to this issue.

The outline of the article will be as follows. First, I will give a brief introduction to Missiology as a theological discipline. Then I will present the case, before I, based on the case, discuss the relation between empirical research and normativity.

---

1   Kari Storstein Haug, *"As you sow, you will reap": Interpreting Proverbs 11:18-31, Psalm 73, and Ecclesiastes 9:1-12 in Light of, and as a Response to Thai Buddhist Interpretations. A Contribution to Christian Buddhist Dialogue*, (PhD thesis, School of Mission and Theology, Stavanger 2008).

What is missiology?[2]

Missiology, as it is understood by the author of this article, is a discipline within theology which studies and critically reflects on the Christian faith and community as they cross cultural and religious frontiers, both locally and globally. This includes both descriptive accounts of and theological reflection on the meeting between Christianity and other religions, and on the different ways Christianity and Christian theology takes form in different cultures and contexts. Further, the discipline reflects critically on the historical and contemporary understanding of the Church's mission, and plays a normative role in formulating contemporary missiological implications for the Church's mission, both globally and locally.

Missiology has no one single method, but utilizes a number of methods depending on the character of research, or the problem one is investigating. Both historical methods, more systematic theological methods, and empirical methods are used in the discipline. In later years there has been a radical increase in studies which combine empirical and more traditional theological methods, mainly systematic-theological methods.

The case

Problem and aims
In the thesis: *'As you sow, you will reap': Interpreting Proverbs 11:18-31, Psalm 73, and Ecclesiastes 9:1-12 in Light of, and as a Response to Thai Buddhist Interpretations. A Contribution to Christian-Buddhist Dialogue*, I

---

2   Missiology as a discipline is designated differently depending on whether it is historically, empirically, systematically or practically oriented. There is an ongoing discussion on the profile and content of the discipline. See for example Jonas P. Adelin Jørgensen and Hans Raun Iversen, "Methodological Plurality and Academic Integrity in Missiology," *Swedish Missiological Themes 93*, no. 3 (2005); Volker Küster, "Toward an Intercultural Theology: Paradigm Shifts in Missiology, Ecumenics, and Comparative Religion," in *Theology and the Religions: A Dialogue*, ed. Viggo Mortensen (Grand Rapids, Mich.: William B. Eerdmans Publishing Company, 2003). Andrew J. Kirk, *What is Mission? Theological Explorations* (London: Darton, Longman and Todd, 1999). Ogbu U. Kalu, Peter Vethanayagamony, and Edmund Kee-Fook Chia, eds., *Mission after Christendom: Emergent Themes in Contemporary Mission* (Louisville, Kentucky: Westminster John Knox Press, 2010), David Kerr, "Missiological Developments from Edinburgh 1910 to Today," *Swedish Missiological Themes 96*, no. 1 (2008).

discuss the *problem* of how Proverbs 11:18-31, Psalm 73 and Ecclesiastes 9:1-12 can be interpreted in light of, and as a response to Thai Buddhist interpretations of the same texts. All three texts belong to the wisdom literature of the Old Testament and relate to a central topic in that literature, namely the expectations about order and justice in life, which can be summarized in the saying "As you sow, you will reap". The text from Proverbs 11 has an optimistic view of causation and expresses a straight forward cause and effect thinking, while the texts from Psalm 73 and Ecclesiastes 9 problematise that there is an inevitable connection between act and consequence. In other words, these two latter texts give, in different ways, expression to the experience that life does not necessarily fit into such a clear cut formula.

The overarching aims of the discussion are: First, to make a contribution toward understanding how interpretation of biblical texts can contribute in the inter-religious encounter between Christianity and Buddhism in Thailand. Second, to explore whether the method used in the thesis, namely of inviting Buddhists to read and interpret biblical texts, and using their interpretations as a starting point for further interpretations and dialogue, could be a fruitful approach both to Bible interpretation and inter-religious dialogue between Christians and Buddhists more generally.

Interviews

In order to be able to answer the problem of how three Old Testament texts can be interpreted in light of, and as a response to Thai Buddhist interpretations of the same texts, material on Thai Buddhists' interpretations of the three texts under study had to be established. This was done through the use of in-depth interviews with 19 Thai Buddhists, during a period of fieldwork in Thailand from June to September 2005.[3] In other words, the focus of my fieldwork was on interviews, nevertheless, I also collected background material on Thai Buddhism through observation, studies at one state university, dialogue with monks and teachers

---

3   The term fieldwork refers to different methods of collecting data in a field, different methods of establishing empirical material. It is the term used in qualitative research to cover the data-collection phase when the researchers leave their desks and go out into the field with the aim to see and learn how people in that respective field understand their world. See for example Sara Delamont, "Ethnography and Participant Observation," in *Qualitative Research Practice*, ed. Clive Seale et al. (London: Sage Publications, 2007).

both at a Buddhist university and at secular universities, and in informal conversations with a wide variety of people.

Within the group of 19 Thai Buddhists, whom I interviewed, I interviewed two main categories of people. The first group I call "professional Buddhists". By this I mean people who have made Buddhism their way of living, i.e. monks and nuns, or people who earn their living as religious specialists – in my material, university teachers in Buddhism. The second group I call "ordinary Buddhists". That is lay persons or ordinary believers, who do not make their living from being religious specialists. The reasons for choosing these two groups were first, that I wanted to secure that some of the interviewees had in-depth knowledge of doctrinal Buddhism, second, to ensure variety with regard to experience in religious practice, and third, to make sure that I had both ordained monks, nuns, and lay people represented in my material. In addition, I was interested in studying if there would be any differences between these two groups with regard to the interpretation of the biblical texts. The main criterion for the selection of interviewees was variety within the two main categories presented above, with regard to age, education, occupation, marital status and gender.

I did the interviews in Thai and was very conscious about, not only what to ask, but how to ask. This means that I consciously employed Thai communicative norms and strategies when interviewing. I will return to this issue in my reflections of normativity later on in the lecture.

Results from the interviews

What were the main results of the interviews? In the following I will briefly sum them up in five points.

First, I gained insight into what themes and issues in the texts the Thai Buddhists found most relevant to discuss, given their background and interests. Generally speaking, the analysis of the Thai Buddhist interpretations has shown that the teaching of *kamma* was the central, but not the only, framework of understanding which the interviewees used in their interpretation.

Second, I learned how the Thai Buddhists I interviewed understood the texts to present and discuss the themes and issues under discussion. Further, in the course of the conversation, the possibility was opened up for learning more about these, or related issues, from a Buddhist point of view, thereby gaining insight into the interviewees' interpretive framework with regard to these issues.

Third, I gained insight into what the Thai Buddhists viewed as main convergences and differences between themes in the texts and their own understanding of them. Not only did their comparisons give deeper insight into the basic framework which informed their reading, but also into questions which Buddhist readers and interpreters had to the texts and their themes.

Fourth, I gained insight into some of the Thai Buddhists' basic pre-understandings regarding the Bible, Christians and Christianity. This made me aware of what kinds of frameworks of understanding of Christianity are activated in the meeting with a Christian text.

Fifth, I learned that in reading the texts the interviewees were very often more concerned with how the insight gained from the texts could be applied in practical life, than wotj discussing the finer points of doctrine.

The use of the empirical material in the wider framework of the thesis

In the last section I briefly indicated some of the main findings which emerged out of the analysis of the interview material, or the empirical component of my research. I will now turn to present how this material was used in the discussion of the problem of the thesis.

The presentation and analysis of Thai Buddhist interpretations of the three texts under study form the first part of my study and the first step towards the answering of the problem of the thesis. The second step, which builds on the results from the analysis in part one, comprises a critical discussion of how the texts, from within their textual contexts, can be interpreted in light of, and as a response to the Thai Buddhist understandings of the texts and their themes.

Therefore, in the second part of the thesis I tried to answer the following questions:
- From the point of view of an interpretation of the texts in their textual context,[4] how do these texts answer the questions and issues raised in the Thai Buddhists' interpretations?
- In view of the answers to the preceding question, and of the result from part one, how can the three texts be interpreted as a response to the Thai Buddhists' own interpretation?

---

4 By textual context I first mean the texts' contexts within the books they belong to, and second the texts' literary contexts in the wisdom literature of the OT.

The argument of the thesis

The answers to these questions contributed towards answering the first problem of my thesis, namely how the three texts from the wisdom literature of the Old Testament can be interpreted in light of, and as a response to Thai Buddhist interpretations of the same texts. I argued that as the analysis showed that the teaching of *kamma* is a central framework of the Thai Buddhist understandings of the texts, an interpretation of the texts in light of, and as a response to Thai Buddhist interpretations must first and foremost relate to the *kamma* framework. Even though there were both a more dogmatically oriented, and a popular oriented understanding at play with regard to what *kamma* is, and how it works, the interviewees to a great extent utilised the framework of *kamma* in similar ways. But, the investigation also revealed that other resources are used by the Thai Buddhists. These include a belief in spirits and fate, personal experiences, cultural values, and their knowledge and understanding of Christian teaching. Therefore, notice must be taken of these alternative or complementary frameworks of understanding, as well as the interviewees' cultural values and their pre-understanding of Christian doctrines related to the themes of the texts. Finally, the analysis of the interviews showed that an interpretation which aims at taking the issues of the Thai interpreters seriously must also consider how the texts can be applied to practical life.

In the discussion of the three texts in question, I then, based on a critical interpretation of the texts in their textual contexts, suggested possible interpretations of the texts which relate to these frameworks of thinking, and the issues raised by the interviewees in their interpretations of the texts.

With regard to the overarching problem of whether the method used in the thesis, namely of inviting Buddhists to read and interpret biblical texts, and using their interpretations as a starting point for further interpretations and dialogue, could be a fruitful approach both to Bible interpretation and interreligious dialogue between Christians and Buddhists more generally, I argued that the method explored is a fruitful approach both to Bible interpretation and inter-religious dialogue in Thailand for the following reasons:

First, as a consequence of gaining insight into what themes and issues in the texts which the Thai Buddhists found most relevant to discuss, one is ensured that the interpretation of the texts and the following discussion and dialogue are related to the context of the dialogue partner and not only reflect the interests of the Christian interpreter.

Second, the insight gained, by using this method, into the interviewees' interpretive framework gives a good basis for an interpretation of the texts which can communicate with Thai Buddhists.

Third, the insight into what kinds of frameworks of understanding with regard to the Bible, Christianity, etc., which are activated in the meeting with a Christian text is of help in the interpretation of the texts, as it enables the interpreter to relate to, comment on, and eventually correct, these pre-understandings in their actual interpretation of the texts.

Additionally, by inviting Thai Buddhists from different walks of life, different ages, gender, and occupations, I argued that my research has demonstrated that one gains a more comprehensive picture of the Thai Buddhist contexts than if one, for example, studies Thai Buddhism only on the basis of books, or dialogue only with official representatives of the Thai *Sangha*. Hence, the Christian interpreter has the opportunity to relate the texts to the actual issues and understandings, not only of religious specialists, but of common people as well. In other words, inviting different Thai Buddhists to a dialogue about biblical texts ensures a more context-sensitive interpretation.

More generally, I argue that my analysis has shown that, by giving Thai Buddhists a voice in the interpretation of the texts, one has a better chance of avoiding the danger of ignoring issues and concerns that are important and relevant to address in a Buddhist context, than if the interpreter sets a strict agenda for the conversation about the texts. In addition, one opens up for a real engagement with the texts and their issues on the part of Buddhist readers, as their point of view is given a central part in the course of the conversation with the Christian partner in the dialogue.

Thus I conclude by arguing that the dissertation has shown that the method explored is a fruitful approach both to Bible interpretation and interreligious dialogue in a Thai context. It has demonstrated its usefulness as an approach in academic research for gaining empirical knowledge of Thai Buddhists' understanding of Christian normative texts, as well as a step in practical Buddhist-Christian dialogue, aimed at establishing Thai Buddhist interpretation of the normative texts of the Other. Hence, based on my research, I argue that in order to interpret biblical texts in a way which both communicates with Thai Buddhists and opens up for further dialogue, it is a fruitful approach to do this interpretation as part of a process of dialogue, where the starting point is how Thai Buddhists read and interpret the biblical texts.

The relation between empirical research and normativity

Constitutive normativity

In planning a research project, empirical as well as pure theoretical research project, there are a number of decisions which must be made with regard to the selection of research topic, theoretical and methodological approaches as well as in regard to the application of research findings, and all these decisions are inevitably connected to norms and values.[5] These decisions might be regarded as normative claims that are constitutive of the research project as a whole. This kind of normativity, which I would argue is present in all research, could consequently be called constitutive normativity.[6]

In other words, in any project there will be a number of normative presuppositions which inform the choice of the problem and the project design. These have consequences for the direction the research takes, as "the way in which one understands a problem determines which particular assumptions will be made and which will not, [which questions will be asked and which will not], and which particular observations will be made and which will not".[7] Therefore, it is important to reflect on the nature of these presuppositions, reveal the implicit decisions, and discuss how they inform the research one is undertaking.

Relating this insight to the case presented in this article it is quite clear that there are important normative presuppositions which have been crucial to the way the problem has been formulated and the project has been designed. In retrospect, I must admit that the project would have benefited from a greater attention to these presuppositions.

The most important presupposition as I see it considers the relation between text and context or religious normativity and social context.[8] In

---

5   Christoph Morgenthaler, "Normative Implications of Designing Empirical Research: Family Research and Reflective Theological Normativity," in *Normativity and Empirical Research in Theology*, ed. Johannes A. van der Ven and Michael Scherer-Rath (Leiden: Brill, 2004). 179, and Ole Riis' contribution in this volume.
6   Cf. Jan-Olav Henriksen's chapter at the beginning of this book.
7   Hans-Georg Ziebertz, "Normativity and Empirical Research in Practical Theology," *Journal of Empirical Theology* 15, no. 1 (2002). 15.
8   For a discussion of the relation between religious normativity and social context, see for example Jaco S. Dreyer, "Theological Normativity: Ideology or Utopia? Reflections on the Possible Contributions of Empirical Research," in *Normativity*

my project, which is concerned with Bible interpretation in a given context, I presuppose that the context matters, not only as a receiver of a transcendent normative message from the Bible, but as an important part of understanding the biblical texts' message or significance. This presupposition thus informed my decision to choose the project design I did for my thesis. As a consequence, I found it necessary to establish a comprehensive material on Thai Buddhist understandings and context, and analyse the interaction between the Thai Buddhist understandings of the biblical texts and an interpretation of the biblical texts in their textual contexts.

One might therefore argue that the reason behind the decision to do fieldwork in a missiological project like mine is part of the constitutive normativity of the project (or the constitutive normativity compels the use of empirical research). If one believes that it is possible to interpret the Bible, or doing theology, independent of actual context, then empirical research might not be regarded as necessary or important in missiology or theological research in general, but if one believes, as I do, that relating to context is a necessary theological task, it becomes crucial to gather empirical knowledge about the context in question.[9] In other words, the possible role of empirical research will be judged differently depending on one's understanding of theological normativity.

Normativity in qualitative oriented research
In the preceding section I have made a case for the unavoidable normativity in all research. I have argued that no research can be done without normative premises or assumptions. In this section I will, on the background of the case presented in this article, briefly relate the discussion to interviews as a method in fieldwork. The focus will be on the interview as a communicative event.

Communicative norms and strategies
I share the basic understanding that interviews are co-operative products of the interaction between the persons participating in the interview.[10]

---

and *Empirical Research in Theology*, ed. Johannes A. van der Ven and Michael Scherer-Rath (Leiden: Brill, 2004).
9 Cf. Harald Hegstad, "Feltarbeid som teologisk metode," Ung Teologi 30, no. 1 (1997). 82.
10 Charles L. Briggs, *Learning How to Ask: A Sociolinguistic Appraisal of the Role of the Interview in Social Science Research*, Studies in the Social and Cultural Foundations of Language, vol. 1 (Cambridge: Cambridge University Press, 1986).

This means that the question and answers in a given interview cannot be seen only as reflecting and referring to situations and facts outside with no relation to the interview situation. They are also dependent on and shaped by the actual interaction that takes place in the frame of an interview situation.[11] This further means that norms and values of communication are bound to influence the interaction between the researcher and the interviewees in many ways, not the least in a situation where the interviewees and the interviewer come from different linguistic, cultural and social backgrounds, as was the case in my research. Thus in order to both create a communication situation which secures a good conversation about the themes and issues which the researcher aims to have elucidated, and in order to analyse the material in a way which takes into account the actual context created by the interview situation, it is crucial to have knowledge about the norms and strategies which govern the different elements in the interview as a communicative event.[12]

Situatedness
Second, the socio-historical location of researcher and informant, including the norms, values and interests that these locations confer upon them, shape their orientation and the way the interview is implemented and analysed. Thus, an important question to consider when doing qualitative research is how both the researcher and informants situatedness influences the interview situation and hence the material collected.[13] The researcher's situatedness might be considered a problem, but in my opinion it is only a problem as long as it is not consciously recognized and taken into account when conducting and analysing the interviews.

102, Tim Rapley, "Interviews," in Qualitative Research Practice, ed. Clive Seale et al. (London: Sage, 2004). 16.

11 See for example Martyn Hammersley and Paul Atkinson, *Ethnography: Principles in Practice,* 3rd ed. (London: Routledge, 2007). 14-19.

12 This is the main argument in Briggs. In my chapter on method, I therefore wrote a lengthy chapter on communicative norms and strategies in Thai society and discussed the consequences of these, both for the actual interview-process and for the analysis of the interviews.

13 I had some years previous to my fieldwork been a missionary in Thailand, hence it was especially important for me to reflect on how my role as a previous missionary and teacher of theology could influence the interviewees' perception of me and how it would influence our communication.

Normative discussions based on empirical material
The third point I want to raise, considers the question of normative discussion based on empirical material.

In doing a project in Missiology, with a constructive aim, which includes empirical research, it is necessary to consider how the empirical material is going to be used in a normative discussion. This is not a question which could be solved as an afterthought, but should be addressed when designing the project, as it is clearly linked to the discussion on the project's constitutive normativity. The case presented in this article had a clear constructive or normative aim, as it aimed at suggesting how three Old Testament wisdom texts could be interpreted in order to both communicate with Thai Buddhists, and open up for further dialogue about themes and issues which the interviewees considered to be important. In other words, the focus was not primarily on how the Thai Buddhists understood the texts, or on how the texts could be understood in their historical, textual contexts, but rather on what their significance could be in the meeting with a contemporary Thai Buddhist context.

Given the question of significance of biblical texts in a contemporary context, I had to consider the relationship between the two sets of textual interpretations in more detail, and clarify what I would consider a valid interpretation of the biblical texts in light of the Thai Buddhist' interpretations. I understand the concept "valid interpretation" of biblical texts in line with Henriksen's definition in *Tegn, Tekst og Tolk*, as an interpretation which is both historically correct and significant for people today.[14] This approach to textual analysis is based on the main presuppositions that there are certain limits to what meanings biblical texts can have, given their historical textual context, but that the texts open up for different interpretations in the meeting between the texts and their contexts, and contemporary readers and their context.[15]

Hence, in order to be able to suggest possible suggestions for valid interpretations of the text in light of, and as a response to the Thai Buddhist context I needed to know how Thai Buddhists would understand the themes and issues in the texts, and I needed to study the texts in their his-

---

14 Jan-Olav Henriksen, ed, *Tegn, Tekst og tolk: Teologisk hermeneutikk i fortid og nåtid* (Oslo: Universitetsforlaget, 1994), 267.
15 Cf. John Barton, *Reading the Old Testament: Method in Biblical Study*, 2nd. ed. (London: Darton, Longman &Todd, 1996), Anthony C. Thiselton, *New Horizons in Hermeneutics: The Theory and Practice of Transforming Biblical Reading* (Grand Rapids, Mich.: Zondervan Publishing House, 1992).

torical textual context, and the research design turned out as I have described it, namely: The empirical research informed the questions put to the historical analysis of the texts. That is, the results of the empirical study of the Thai Buddhist text interpretations were decisive for the formulation of the questions I addressed the texts with. Then I investigated whether and how the texts might be regarded as responding to these questions, given the textual contexts of the texts.

It could be objected, as it was at my defence, that this way of using empirical research could be seen as a Eurocentric evaluation of Thai readings of the texts. It might look like I evaluated the Thai Buddhist interpretation as "flawed", "less good", from the perspective of a quite Eurocentric historical-critical perspective. Against this objection I would argue that my aim was not to evaluate the Thai Buddhist interpretations as good or bad, flawed or unflawed. I have tried to present the Buddhist interpretations as precisely and objectively as possible. Their interpretations have, however, formed the basis for a normative discussion of how the texts could be interpreted in a way that both take seriously the themes and issues raised by the Buddhist interpreters, and respect the horizon of the text.

This further invites the question how to decide which interpretation is a valid interpretation. The aim to interpret the texts in their textual contexts raises the question if it is at all possible to gain an historical understanding of the texts, or whether all interpretations are totally dependent on the interpreter's own cultural lenses. In my view the background of an interpreter will influence his or her understanding of a text. Hence, a completely unbiased and objective reading of texts is not possible. Even if it is a fact that different perspectives lead to different interpretations, I would argue that this doesn't have to lead to pure perspectivism. I would claim that there are more or less qualified and adequate interpretations of biblical texts. It is, however, not one culture, or a western elite, who decides what is a valid interpretation of biblical texts. What could be possible valid interpretations in different contexts has to be argued and reasoned for within an academic theological discourse.[16] I intended my discussion to be part of that discourse, and put to the table a suggestion for

---

16 For a discussion of the importance of academic discourse for normative theological argumentation, see Jan-Olav Henriksen, "Om forholdet mellom teologi og religionsvitenskap - sett fra teologiens ståsted," in *Danning, identitet og dialog: Festskrift til Jan Ove Ulstein og Per Magne Aadnanes*, ed. Birger Løvlie, Ralph Meier, and Arne Redse (Trondheim: Tapir Akademisk Forlag, 2009).

what could be possible interpretations of these three texts in a Buddhist context.

Conclusion

In this article, I have discussed some of the methodological challenges related to doing qualitative oriented research and combining empirical material and normative theological discussion. I have made a case for the unavoidable normativity in all phases of the research, as there in any research are a number of decisions which must be made with regard to the selection of research topic, theoretical and methodological approaches as well as to the application of research findings, and all these decisions are inevitable connected to norms and values.

Second, I have argued that the possible role of empirical research in a theological project will be judged differently depending on one's understanding of theological normativity. It is my contention that all interpretations of Christianity is formed by, and need to take into account the context. Hence, based on such an understanding, in a theological project using empirical research, the empirical material is an integrated part in the overarching theological discussion.

Third, and finally, I have tried to show that the way in which the empirical material is integrated and used in an actual research project, depends on the decisions made in the formulation of the problem, and the consequent project design. These decisions should be transparent and their underlying presuppositions should be argued for.

References

Barton, John. *Reading the Old Testament: Method in Biblical Study*. 2nd. ed. London: Darton, Longman &Todd, 1996.

Briggs, Charles L. *Learning How to Ask: A Sociolinguistic Appraisal of the Role of the Interview in Social Science Research*. Vol. 1 Studies in the Social and Cultural Foundations of Language. Cambridge: Cambridge University Press, 1986.

Delamont, Sara. "Ethnography and Participant Observation." In *Qualitative Research Practice*, ed. Clive Seale, Giampietro Gobo, Jaber F Gubrium and David Silverman, 205-217. London: Sage Publications, 2007.

Dreyer, Jaco S. "Theological Normativity: Ideology or Utopia? Reflections on the Possible Contributions of Empirical Research." In *Normativity and Empirical Research in Theology*, ed. Johannes A. van der Ven and Michael Scherer-Rath, 3-16. Leiden: Brill, 2004.

Hammersley, Martyn, and Paul Atkinson. *Ethnography: Principles in Practice*. 3rd ed. London: Routledge, 2007.

Haug, Kari Storstein. ""As you sow, you will reap": Interpreting Proverbs 11:18-31, Psalm 73, and Ecclesiastes 9:1-12 in Light of, and as a Response to Thai Buddhist Interpretations. A Contribution to Christian Buddhist Dialogue." PhD thesis, School of Mission and Theology, Stavanger 2008.

Hegstad, Harald. "Feltarbeid som teologisk metode." *Ung Teologi* 30, no. 1 (1997): 77-82.

Henriksen, Jan-Olav. "Om forholdet mellom teologi og religionsvitenskap - sett fra teologiens ståsted." In *Danning, identitet og dialog: Festskrift til Jan Ove Ulstein og Per Magne Aadnanes*, ed. Birger Løvlie, Ralph Meier and Arne Redse, 89-101. Trondheim: Tapir Akademisk Forlag, 2009.

Henriksen, Jan-Olav, ed. *Tegn, Tekst og Tolk: Teologisk hermeneutikk i fortid og nåtid*. Oslo: Universitetsforlaget, 1994.

Henriksen, Jan-Olav. "Normative dimensions in empirical research on religion, values and society", in this volume.

Jørgensen, Jonas P. Adelin, and Hans Raun Iversen. "Methodological Plurality and Academic Integrity in Missiology." *Swedish Missiological Themes* 93, no. 3 (2005): 311-314.

Kalu, Ogbu U., Peter Vethanayagamony, and Edmund Kee-Fook Chia, eds. *Mission after Christendom: Emergent Themes in Contemporary Mission*. Louisville, Kentucky: Westminster John Knox Press, 2010.

Kerr, David. "Missiological Developments from Edinburgh 1910 to Today." *Swedish Missiological Themes* 96, no. 1 (2008): 9-26.

Kirk, Andrew J. *What is Mission? Theological Explorations*. London: Darton, Longman and Todd, 1999.

Küster, Volker. "Toward an Intercultural Theology: Paradigm Shifts in Missiology, Ecumenics, and Comparative Religion." In *Theology and the Religions: A Dialogue*, ed. Viggo Mortensen, 171-184. Grand Rapids, Mich.: William B. Eerdmans Publishing Company, 2003.

Morgenthaler, Christoph. "Normative Implications of Designing Empirical Research: Family Research and Reflective Theological Normativity." In *Normativity and Empirical Research in Theology*, ed. Johannes A. van der Ven and Michael Scherer-Rath, 179-198. Leiden: Brill, 2004.

Rapley, Tim. "Interviews." In *Qualitative Research Practice*, ed. Clive Seale, Giampietro Gobo, Jaber F Gubrium and David Silverman, 15-33. London: Sage, 2004.

Riis, Ole. "Normative Evaluations and Components in Sociological Research: The Contributions of Critical Theory." Paper given at *Religion Values Society Interdisciplinary Research School*. Metochi, Lesbos, 2010.

Thiselton, Anthony C. *New Horizons in Hermeneutics: The Theory and Practice of Transforming Biblical Reading*. Grand Rapids, Mich.: Zondervan Publishing House, 1992.

Ziebertz, Hans-Georg. "Normativity and Empirical Research in Practical Theology." *Journal of Empirical Theology* 15, no. 1 (2002): 5-18.

Gijsbert van den Brink

Philosophy of Science for Theologians
An Introduction

Frankfurt am Main, Berlin, Bern, Bruxelles, New York, Oxford, Wien, 2009.
299 pp.
Contributions to Philosophical Theology.
Edited by Vincent Brümmer, Gijsbert van den Brink and Marcel Sarot. Vol. 12
ISBN 978-3-631-56951-1 · hardback € 49.80*

This book tells the story of the philosophy of science from its inception in the aftermath of the first World War to its current stage, and relates this story to the status of theology. In doing so, it fills a remarkable gap in the literature. The unexpected resurgence of religious issues in often heated discussions since the beginning of the 21st century gave a new urgency to the question of the academic treatment of religion(s). Is it still adequate to allow for the academic study of religion only in a distanced and matter-of-fact way, without people's own views of life being brought into play and confronted with each other? Or can we also have a viable form of theology that starts from a basic religious commitment, but nevertheless fully satisfies academic standards? There is a wide debate on topics like these – but seldom this debate is conducted in a way that is informed by the state of the art in the philosophy of science.

Contents: History of the philosophy of science · Theology as an academic discipline · Science and religion · The idea of progress · Logical positivism · Karl Popper · Thomas Kuhn · Imre Lakatos · Theory-ladenness of observation · Perspectivity · Theory of modal spheres · Christian faith and spirituality · Wolfhart Pannenberg · Nancey Murphy · Ian Barbour

Frankfurt am Main · Berlin · Bern · Bruxelles · New York · Oxford · Wien
Distribution: Verlag Peter Lang AG
Moosstr. 1, CH-2542 Pieterlen
Telefax 0041(0)32/3761727

*The €-price includes German tax rate
Prices are subject to change without notice
Homepage http://www.peterlang.de